The Voice of the Ch

Uwe Michael Lang

The Voice of the Church at Prayer

Reflections on Liturgy and Language

IGNATIUS PRESS SAN FRANCISCO

Cover art:
Saint Peter, from an illuminated manuscript
Fra Angelico (1387–1455)

Cover design by Roxanne Mei Lum

ISBN 978-1-58617-720-1
Library of Congress Control Number 2011940930
Printed in the United States of America ♾

CONTENTS

ABBREVIATIONS

CCCM	Corpus Christianorum. Continuatio Mediaevalis. Turnhout: Brepols, 1966–.
CCSL	Corpus Christianorum. Series Latina. Turnhout: Brepols, 1953–.
CSEL	Corpus Scriptorum Ecclesiasticorum Latinorum. Vienna: Geroldi, then Tempksy, 1866–.
PG	Patrologiae Cursus Completus, accurante J.-P. Migne. Series Graeca. 166 vols. Paris: Petit-Montrouge, 1857–1883.
PL	Patrologiae Cursus Completus, accurante J.-P. Migne. Series Latina. 221 vols. Paris: J.-P. Migne, 1844–1865.
SC	Sources Chrétiennes. Paris: Cerf, 1941–.

Missale Romanum 1570	*Missale Romanum ex decreto Sacrosancti Concilii Tridentini restitutum Pii V Pont. Max. iussu editum.* Rome: Apud heredes Bartholomei Faletti, Joannem Variscum & socios, 1570.
Missale Romanum 1962	*Missale Romanum ex decreto SS. Concilii Tridentini restitutum Summorum Pontificum cura recognitum.* Editio typica. Vatican City: Typis Polyglottis Vaticanis, 1962.
Missale Romanum 1970	*Missale Romanum ex decreto Sacrosancti Oecumenici Concilii Vaticani II*

	instauratum auctoritate Pauli PP. VI promulgatum. Editio typica. Vatican City: Typis Polyglottis Vaticani, 1970.
Missale Romanum 2008	*Missale Romanum ex decreto Sacrosancti Oecumenici Concilii Vaticani II instauratum auctoritate Pauli PP. VI promulgatum Ioannis Pauli PP. II cura recognitum*. Editio typica tertia, reimpressio emendata. Vatican City: Typis Vaticanis, 2002.
Roman Missal 1974	*Roman Missal: Revised by Decree of the Second Vatican Council and Published by Authority of Pope Paul VI*. London: Collins Liturgical, 1974.
Roman Missal 2011	*Roman Missal: Renewed by Decree of the Most Holy Second Ecumenical Council of the Vatican, Promulgated by Authority of Pope Paul VI and Revised at the Direction of Pope John Paul II*. Totowa, N.J.: Catholic Book Publishing, 2011.

INTRODUCTION

This is a propitious time to write a book about liturgy and language. Benedict XVI has placed the sacred liturgy at the heart of his pontificate, and the decisions he has taken in this regard are of lasting significance both on a theoretical and on a practical level. The Pope, noted for his own scholarly contributions on the subject, explains his rationale in *Theology of the Liturgy*, the eleventh volume of his collected writings, which was the first one to be published, at his express wish, in 2008.[1] In his preface, dated June 29, 2008, the Solemnity of Saints Peter and Paul, Benedict XVI observes that this choice was an obvious one to him, because the liturgy has been central to his life ever since his childhood and it is the heart of his theological work. However, there is another reason to begin the series with the volume on the liturgy: the editorial project aspires to reflect the order of priorities of the Second Vatican Council. The Holy Father draws attention to the fact that the Council's first document was the Constitution on the Sacred Liturgy, *Sacrosanctum concilium*. In his view, this was not just a pragmatic decision that seemed expedient in the given circumstances; rather, it reflects the right ordering of the Church's life and mission:

> By beginning with the theme of "liturgy", the primacy of God, the priority of the theme "God", was unequivocally

[1] J. Ratzinger, *Theologie der Liturgie: Die sakramentale Begründung christlicher Existenz*, Gesammelte Schriften 11 (Freiburg im Breisgau: Herder, 2008). The English version is being prepared by Ignatius Press.

> brought to light. God first: this is meant by beginning with the liturgy. When the focus is not on God, everything else loses its orientation. The words of the Benedictine rule ... "Let nothing be put before the Work of God" (43, 3) apply specifically to monasticism, but as an order of priority, they are also true for the life of the Church and of each and every one ... in his own way.[2]

Pope Benedict then recalls a theme he has explored in his various writings on the liturgy, the fullness of the meaning of "orthodoxy":

> It is perhaps useful to recall that in the term "orthodoxy," the second half of the word, *doxa*, does not mean "opinion", but "glory" (*Herrlichkeit*): this is not a matter of a correct "opinion" about God, but of a proper way of glorifying him, of responding to him. For this is the fundamental question of the man who begins to understand himself in the correct way: How should I encounter God? Thus, learning the right way of adoration—of orthodoxy—is the first gift the faith bestows upon us.[3]

In his homilies and discourses, and in a special way in his own liturgical celebrations, Benedict XVI has consistently followed this order of priorities and has conveyed to a worldwide public his profound theological concern, which he has expressed in his many writings on the subject, namely, that the sacred liturgy must be a reflection of the glory of God. This holds true especially for the celebration of Holy Mass, where the Paschal Mystery of Christ's Passion, death,

---

[2] Benedict XVI, "Zum Eröffnungsband meiner Schriften", in Ratzinger, *Theologie der Liturgie*, 5–6. English translation by M. Sherry (slightly modified), http://chiesa.espresso.repubblica.it/articolo/208933?eng=y (accessed on August 11, 2010).

[3] Benedict XVI, "Zum Eröffnungsband meiner Schriften", 6.

and Resurrection is made present ever anew in sacramental form.

Liturgy matters—not only because, from a purely empirical perspective, it is at Sunday Mass that the vast majority of practicing Catholics experience the Church. More profoundly, the worship of God is "the summit toward which the activity of the Church is directed; at the same time it is the font from which all her power flows",[4] as *Sacrosanctum concilium* affirms. In the liturgy, especially in the holy sacrifice of the Eucharist, "the work of our redemption is accomplished", as an ancient prayer of the Roman rite of Mass declares. Moreover, divine worship manifests to the world "the mystery of Christ and the real nature of the true Church".[5] In other words, the Church's liturgy is an expression of and witness to her infallible faith, and it should help us to understand in a way surpassing all verbalization that our aspirations for goodness, for truth, for beauty, and for love are grounded in the all-surpassing reality of God.[6]

Language is obviously an essential aspect of the liturgy, but there are more specific reasons why this subject is pertinent in the present time. In the first place, there is a renewed interest in Latin, which has been the liturgical language of the Christian West ever since late antiquity. The Fathers of the Second Vatican Council granted a significant extension of the use of the vernacular in the Catholic liturgy, which

---

[4] Second Vatican Council, Constitution on the Sacred Liturgy *Sacrosanctum concilium* (December 4, 1963), no. 10.

[5] Ibid., no. 2; the quotation is taken from the *secreta* of the Ninth Sunday after Pentecost (Extraordinary Form of the Roman Rite), now also the *oratio super oblata* for the Second Sunday *per Annum* and for the Mass of the Last Supper on Maundy Thursday in the Ordinary Form.

[6] Cf. the insightful work of J. Robinson, *The Mass and Modernity: Walking to Heaven Backward* (San Francisco: Ignatius Press, 2005).

had been used to a very limited extent before, with the primary motive of promoting the "fully conscious and active participation" of the people in the sacred rites.[7] However, they did not envisage a general and total replacement of Latin as the liturgical language of the Catholic Church with the mother tongue.

Even today, the Latin language holds primacy of place as the liturgical language of the Roman rite, although most celebrations are in fact held in the vernacular.[8] The official editions (*editiones typicae*) of the liturgical books in the Roman rite are published in Latin and then translated into the local languages. Latin has remained the language of papal liturgies, above all in Rome, when thousands of pilgrims from all over the world gather together. More recently, Benedict XVI has extended the use of Latin in his celebrations as Supreme Pontiff: on his visits outside Rome, Latin is now commonly used for the chants of the Ordinary of the Mass and for the Eucharistic Prayer (that is, from the Preface to the *Pater Noster*). The present Pope has also called for a greater prominence of the Latin liturgy in the formation of priests and for its extended use especially at, but by no means limited to, international gatherings.[9]

The strongest impulse for a renaissance of Latin as a liturgical language was given with the Motu Proprio *Summorum*

---

[7] *Sacrosanctum concilium*, no. 14.

[8] Cf. John Paul II, Apostolic Letter *Dominicae cenae* (February 24, 1980), *Acta Apostolicae Sedis* 72 (1980): 113–48, no. 10: "The Roman Church has special obligations towards Latin, the splendid language of ancient Rome, and she must manifest them whenever the occasion presents itself." Unless otherwise indicated, the English translation for all Church documents quoted has been taken from the Vatican website (http://www.vatican.va); full web addresses for individual documents can be found below in the bibliography.

[9] Benedict XVI, Post-Synodical Apostolic Exhortation *Sacramentum caritatis* (February 22, 2007), *Acta Apostolicae Sedis* 99 (2007): 105–80, no. 62.

Pontificum of July 7, 2007, which lifted previous restrictions that applied to the *Missale Romanum* of 1962 and the other liturgical books in use before 1970. They now constitute the "Extraordinary Form", or *usus antiquior* (older use), which, together with the "Ordinary Form", is an expression of the one Roman rite.[10] While the reach of this decision goes far beyond the question of language, it greatly extends the presence of Latin in the Church's divine worship. Moreover, Pope Benedict notes in his explanatory letter to the bishops accompanying the Motu Proprio that through the coexistence of the two forms, which can be "mutually enriching", "the celebration of the Mass according to the Missal of Paul VI will be able to demonstrate, more powerfully than has been the case hitherto, the sacrality which attracts many people to the former usage."[11] Obviously, the liturgical language contributes much to the sacred and stable character of the *usus antiquior*, and hence the Pope's statement should also be considered a call for the recovery of Latin in the "Ordinary Form".

There is a second reason why historical and theological reflections on liturgy and language are topical: the question of translation. In the wake of the Second Vatican Council, the new liturgical books were translated into the many

[10] Benedict XVI, Apostolic Letter *Summorum Pontificum* given Motu Proprio (July 7, 2007), *Acta Apostolicae Sedis* 99 (2007): 777–81; (unofficial) English translation: http://www.catholic-ew.org.uk/content/download/5724/39439/file/Apostolic_Letter_Summorum_Pontificum.pdf. See now also Pontifical Commission *Ecclesia Dei*, Instruction on the Application of the Apostolic Letter *Summorum Pontificum* given Motu Proprio *Universae Ecclesiae* (April 30, 2011), in *L'Osservatore Romano*, May 14, 2011, 4–5.

[11] Benedict XVI, Letter to the Bishops on the Occasion of the Publication of the Apostolic Letter *Summorum Pontificum* given Motu Proprio (July 7, 2007), *Acta Apostolicae Sedis* 99 (2007): 795–99.

vernaculars of the world. The instruction *Liturgiam authenticam*, issued by the Congregation for Divine Worship and the Discipline of the Sacraments in 2001, marked the beginning of a thoroughgoing assessment and revision of these translations.[12] This process is of particular consequence in the English-speaking world, for reasons that will be addressed in this study, and it has already yielded what is perhaps its most important fruit, the new *Roman Missal*, which has been implemented in most Anglophone countries in the course of the year 2011.

The title of this book is borrowed from *Liturgiam authenticam*, which insists that "liturgical texts should be considered as the voice of the Church at prayer (*vox Ecclesiae orantis*), rather than of only particular congregations or individuals."[13] While the following chapters will unfold some of the implications of this principle, they are not conceived as a comprehensive history or a systematic theological treatment of liturgy and language. Rather, I intend to address several significant moments in the development of this complex and subtle relationship, beginning in chapter 1 with a discussion of biblical language and the formation of a Latin Christian idiom. The following chapters 2 and 3 are dedicated to the origins and the characteristics of Latin as the sacred language of the Roman liturgy. In chapter 4, a brief account of the transition from late antiquity to the Middle Ages is given. Particular attention is paid to Saint Thomas Aquinas' theological considerations on the subject of liturgy and language in chapter 5. Finally, chapter 6 follows

---

[12] Congregation for Divine Worship and the Discipline of the Sacraments, Fifth Instruction for the Right Implementation of the Constitution on the Sacred Liturgy *Liturgiam authenticam* (March 28, 2001), *Acta Apostolicae Sedis* 93 (2001): 685–726.

[13] *Liturgiam authenticam*, no. 27.

the history of Latin and the vernacular in the modern age up to the present day.

This book has been long in the making and in many ways represents a synthesis of my work in the last few years. Some of the material has been presented previously in papers and publications;[14] it has been revised and now forms part of a whole that will in turn shed light on particular issues. I would like to express my gratitude to all who have contributed to its writing with their encouragement and criticism, especially Michael P. Foley, whose observations have been invaluable. Thanks are also due to Maria Caterina Calabrò, Richard Dobbins, and Martin Stamnestrø for their help in preparing the typescript. This book is dedicated with affection to my confreres in the Oratory of Saint Philip Neri in London: *alter alterius onera portate, et sic adimplebitis legem Christi* (Gal 6:2).

[14] See esp. "Rhetoric of Salvation: The Origins of Latin as the Language of the Roman Liturgy", in *The Genius of the Roman Liturgy: Historical Diversity and Spiritual Reach: Proceedings of the 2006 Oxford CIEL Colloquium*, ed. U. M. Lang (Chicago: Hillenbrand Books, 2010), 22–44, and "Found in Translation: The 'Sacral Vernacular' of the New English Translation of the Roman Missal", *The Priest: The Journal of the Australian Confraternity of Catholic Clergy* 25 (2010): 20–27 and 33.

I

THE LANGUAGE OF HOLY SCRIPTURE

The Lord's Way of Speaking

A few years ago, the American patristics scholar Robert Louis Wilken published in the journal *First Things* an insightful article with the title "The Church's Way of Speaking". At the beginning of the article, Wilken draws attention to a striking phrase from Saint Augustine's *Confessions*: "in dominico eloquio" (in the Lord's way of speaking).[1] The phrase occurs in book 9 of the *Confessions*, where Augustine recounts the events after his dramatic conversion experience in a Milanese garden in the summer of the year 386. After he retired from his chair of rhetoric, partly because he suffered from poor health, partly because he wanted to prepare for baptism, Augustine turned to Saint Ambrose, the Bishop of Milan, to ask for "his advice as to which of your books it was best for me to read so that I might be the more ready and fit for the reception of so great a grace". The Bishop recommended the book of the prophet Isaiah, the reading of which caused Augustine some perplexity, as he wrote in retrospection:

[1] R. L. Wilken, "The Church's Way of Speaking", *First Things* 154 (August/September 2005): 27.

> I believe it was because Isaiah announces, more clearly than others, the Gospel and the calling of the Gentiles. However, because I could not understand the first passage of the book and because I thought the rest would be like it, I laid it aside, to take it up again when I was better practiced in the Lord's way of speaking.[2]

Ambrose directed his candidate for baptism to Isaiah, who, according to Saint Jerome, was not only a prophet, but also an evangelist and an apostle.[3] We can relate to this tribute by the great exegete of Christian antiquity if we think of the well-known passages from this biblical book that are cited in the New Testament, indeed by Jesus himself (see above all Isaiah 61:1–2 in Luke 4:18–19, but also, for instance, Isaiah 56:7 in Matthew 21:12–13, Mark 11:17, and Luke 19:46) and of those that are used in the Church's liturgy, especially during the seasons of Advent and Christmas (from chapters 7, 9, 40) and in Holy Week (from chapters 42 and 53).

However, our familiarity with these prophecies from their Christian liturgical setting should not make us oblivious to the fact that Isaiah is, in large parts, daunting and difficult to understand. Augustine's own struggle with this biblical book, in turn, evokes the story of the Ethiopian eunuch and the Deacon Philip in Acts 8:26–39. Anyone who opens its first chapter, as presumably Augustine did, can sympathize with his perplexity: "Ah, sinful nation, a people laden with iniquity, offspring of evildoers, sons who deal corruptly! They have

---

[2] ". . . at ille iussit Esaiam prophetam, credo, quod prae ceteris evangelii vocationisque gentium sit praenuntiator apertior. verum tamen ego primam huius lectionem non intellegens totumque talem arbitrans distuli repetendum exercitatior in dominico eloquio"; Augustine, *Confessiones* IX, 5, 13: Augustine, *Confessions: Introduction, Text, and Commentary*, ed. J.J. O'Donnell, 3 vols. (Oxford: Clarendon Press, 1992), ad loc.

[3] Jerome, *Comm. in Is.* I, 2: CCSL 73:1–3.

forsaken the LORD, they have despised the Holy One of Israel, they are utterly estranged" (Is 1:4). We need to remember that Augustine was educated in the classical tradition and that his sense of style was formed by the poetry of Virgil. Earlier in his life, in Carthage, he had begun to read the Scriptures but was repelled by their poor literary style, which could not match the *Tulliana dignitas*, the dignity of Cicero.[4] No wonder, then, that Augustine was puzzled by this talk about "sinful nation", "Holy One of Israel", "daughter of Zion". This must have sounded to him like a barbarian voice coming from a remote and backward province of the Roman Empire. Augustine was also influenced by Neoplatonic philosophy and must have been embarrassed by the crude anthropomorphisms that make the God of Israel say "I will vent my wrath on my enemies" and "turn my hand against you".

And yet, this cultivated professor of rhetoric recognized in this book "the Lord's way of speaking" and acknowledged that he had to be schooled in it. Augustine saw that he had to learn a new language, the language of Holy Scripture and the Church. In order to become a Christian, he had to be able to understand and speak this new language. Augustine realized that the instruction of catechumens means much more than teaching the basics of faith and morals, although this is an essential part of it. The sacraments of initiation liberate those who receive them from the bondage of sin and death and lead them to a new life as children of God, members of the body of Christ, which is the Church, and temples of the Holy Spirit. This new creation is understood and interpreted by means of the language of salvation, which is shaped by the use of the Holy Scriptures and handed down in the Church.

[4] Augustine, *Confessiones* III, 5, 9: ed. O'Donnell, ad loc.

This point holds for the early Church as well as for our own time, as then-Cardinal Joseph Ratzinger observed:

> No one lives alone. The reference to the connection between gospel and culture is meant to make this clear. Becoming a Christian requires a lived context in which cultural healing and transformation can be accomplished. Evangelization is never merely intellectual communication; it is a process of experience, the purification and transformation of our lives, and for this to happen, company along the way [*Weggemeinschaft*] is needed.[5]

An essential element of this "common pilgrimage", which is a characteristic of the Church in this world, is a common language, in which the process of transformation can be

---

[5] J. Ratzinger, "Communication and Culture: New Methods of Evangelization in the Third Millennium", in *On the Way to Jesus Christ*, trans. M. J. Miller (San Francisco: Ignatius Press, 2005), 50. Shortly after his election to the papacy, Benedict XVI returned to this important aspect of the Catholic faith in a remarkable, improvised question-and-answer session with the Roman clergy: "It seems to me important firstly to awaken this intention to believe with the Church, even if personally someone may not yet have assimilated many particulars. It is necessary to have this will to believe with the Church, to have trust that this Church—the community not only of 2,000 years of pilgrimage of the people of God, but the community that embraces heaven and earth, the community where all the righteous of all times are therefore present—that this Church enlivened by the Holy Spirit truly carries within the 'compass' of the Spirit and therefore is the true subject of faith. The individual, then, is inserted into this subject, adheres to it, and so, even if he or she is still not completely penetrated by this, the person has trust and participates in the faith of the Church, wants to believe with the Church. To me, this seems like our lifelong pilgrimage: to arrive with our thought, our affections, with our entire life at the communion of faith. We can offer this to everyone, so that little by little one can identify and especially take this step over and over again to trust in the faith of the Church, to insert themselves in this pilgrimage of faith, so as to receive the light of faith": Benedict XVI, *Address to the Clergy of Rome* (May 13, 2005); see also his *Address to the Italian Bishops Taking Part in the 54th Assembly of the Italian Bishops' Conference* (May 30, 2005).

expressed. This is so important, because language is more than just a means of communication; it also "organizes" our intellectual and affective experiences and is constitutive of our social and cultural identity:

> Man is never alone, he bears the stamp of a community that provides him with patterns of thinking, feeling, and acting. This system of notions and thought patterns that preconditions the individual human being goes by the name of culture. The first and foremost component of culture is the common language.[6]

The German philosopher Robert Spaemann underscores the significance of a common language for public life, arguing that even in pluralistic societies there is need for a basic "common language". This need not necessarily be a language in the linguistic sense. Switzerland, for example, has four official languages now, but in another, nonlinguistic sense it has a common language, that is, in the sense that its people understand approximately the same meaning by the same or by corresponding words. This implies that there is a certain common repertoire of associations that are connected with important concepts in public life. Problems arise, not so much because of linguistic differences, but because of ideological differences that put a burden on the life of the community and reduce the possibility of mutual understanding. This commonality of associations is based on a common stock of memories. In the family there is the "Do you remember . . ." (Weißt du noch . . .), which draws all its members into the common conversation. Nations also have such a common stock of memories, which is invoked, for instance, on public feast

[6] Ratzinger, "Communication and Culture", 43–44.

days. Conversely, a radically pluralistic society is hardly able to celebrate common festivals.[7]

Spaemann's insightful comments are relevant for ecclesial life, because the Church is also a *polis* that needs a common language. As an image of the Church, Augustine used the *civitas Dei*, the city of God. The Church as a *polis* or *civitas* also has a common "way of speaking" that transcends national language and has a universal character. This common language is familiar to us: Father, Son, and Holy Spirit; faith, hope, and charity; sin and forgiveness; the Kingdom of God, Lamb of God, Passion, and so on. In addition, there are the many names of persons and places that are linked with associations in the Jewish and Christian vocabulary: Jerusalem, Mount of Olives, Zion, Bethlehem, Golgotha, Abraham, Isaac and Jacob, Joseph and Mary, Peter and Paul, and so forth. Wherever the Gospel was preached, this language, rooted in the Sacred Scriptures, is understood by Christians, whether they speak English, German, Russian, Arabic, or any other tongue. Thus Robert Wilken concludes in his above-mentioned article on "The Church's Way of Speaking":

> The faith, then, is embedded in language. It is not a set of abstract beliefs or ideas, but a world of shared associations and allusions with its own beauty and sonority, inner cohesion and logic, emotional and rhetorical power. The Church's way of speaking is a collection of the words and images that have formed the thinking and actions of those who have known Christ. The faith they confessed cannot be divorced from the words they used, nor the words uprooted from the lives of their speakers. Christian thinking is inescapably historical. . . . Without the distinctive Christian

[7] See R. Spaemann, "Europa—Wertegemeinschaft oder Rechtsordnung?", *Transit—Europäische Revue* 21/2001: 172–73.

> language there can be no full Christian life, no faithful handing on of the faith to the next generation.[8]

Augustine was highly conscious of this fact and, in the passage cited at the beginning of this chapter, wrote about his need to become familiar with the *dominicum eloquium*. Earlier in the ninth book of the *Confessions*, Augustine reflected upon relinquishing his chair of rhetoric in Milan and retiring to a country villa in Cassiciacum, on the slopes of the Alps:

> You released my tongue, as you had already released my heart; and I praised you with joy, and went with my friends to the country. What I got done there in writing was now devoted to your service, though in this time of rest, it was still as if I were panting from my exertions in the school of pride. These were the books in which I engaged in dialogue with my friends, and those in soliloquy before you alone.[9]

These lines were written sometime between 397 and 401, that is, more than ten years after the events recorded here. Thus it is with hindsight that Augustine realized that, even after his conversion experience, traces of his secular ambition remained in him. The "school of pride" (*superbiae schola*), to which he still saw himself indebted, showed not so much in the contents of his writing of this period in his life but, rather, in its style. During his retreat in Cassiciacum, he had not yet mastered the forms of expression used by Latin Christians in his age, a language that was formed by the use

---

[8] Wilken, "Church's Way of Speaking", 29.

[9] Augustine, *Confessiones* IX, 4, 7: ed. O'Donnell, ad loc.: "eruisti linguam meam unde iam erueras cor meum, et benedicebam tibi gaudens, profectus in villam cum meis omnibus. Ibi quid egerim in litteris iam quidem servientibus tibi, sed adhuc superbiae scholam tamquam in pausatione anhelantibus, testantur libri disputati cum praesentibus et cum ipso me solo coram te."

of the Bible and of the liturgy. As Augustine said of himself in the following section of the *Confessions*: "I was still uninstructed in your true love, a catechumen on holiday in the country with Alypius, a catechumen like myself."[10]

Augustine's keen awareness of the use of language and its inherent problems remained with him until the end of his life, when in the year 426, he began to read through his earlier writings and put together a substantial work of revisions, known as *Retractationes*. In its prologue, Augustine noted in particular that he did not want to leave unedited the works he had composed as a catechumen. These were written already under Christian inspiration but were still indebted to the literary forms of the secular schools.[11] What Augustine found inappropriate in his early works becomes clear in the first four chapters of the *Retractationes*. There is virtually nothing in the content that he regrets: all of his retractions concern particular phrasing or the use of words with a strong pagan connotation, such as *fortuna* and *omen*, in his dialogues *Contra academicos, De beata vita*, and *De ordine*, written in Cassiciacum when he was preparing for baptism.[12] During his remarkable career as a preacher and author of many theological writings, Augustine became ever more aware of the Church's own way of speaking, which he coined

[10] Augustine, *Confessiones* IX, 4, 8: ed. O'Donnell, ad loc.: "Rudis in germano amore tuo, catechumenus in villa cum catechumeno Alypio feriatus."

[11] Augustine, *Retractationes*, prol. 3: CCSL 57:6: "Nec illa sane praetereo quae cathecuminus iam, licet relicta spe quam terrenam gerebam, sed adhuc saecularium litterarum inflatus consuetudine scripsi."

[12] Augustine, *Retractationes* I, 1–4: CCSL 57:7–11. Cf. C. Mohrmann, "Comment saint Augustin s'est familiarisé avec le latin des chrétiens", in *Études sur le latin des chrétiens*, 4 vols., Storia e letteratura 65, 87, 103, 143 (Rome: Edizioni di Storia e Letteratura, 1961–1977), 1:383–89. Mohrmann also notes developments in Augustine's syntax and grammar; see C. Mohrmann, "Saint Augustin écrivain", in *Études sur le latin des chrétiens*, 2:247–75.

"ecclesiastica loquendi consuetudo" or "ritus loquendi ecclesiasticus".[13]

Augustine's testimony confirms that by the early fifth century there were well-established forms of Christian discourse in the Latin language that were expressed in the teaching, worship, and organization of the Church and that had their distinctive features compared to common discourse in late antiquity.

The Question of "Christian Latin"

The Nijmwegen School of Josef Schrijnen, Christine Mohrmann, and their students proposed the idea of Christian Latin as a "special language" (*Sondersprache*), which is marked by particularities in morphology, lexis, and syntax. According to this theory, the special or group language of the early Christian communities is characterized by many elements of "Vulgar Latin", which would reflect the humble social origins of their members as well as their strong bonds with one another, covering every aspect of life. Mohrmann also sees in the first three centuries a period of "rigorism", when Christians sought to express the newness and otherness of their faith in non-classical linguistic forms.[14] This distance from received Latinity may even have been an obstacle for the diffusion of Christian authors among a pagan readership. This interpretation would seem to be confirmed by

[13] Augustine, *Enarrationes in psalmos* 93, 3: CCSL 39:1303; *De civitate Dei* X, 21: CCSL 47:295; see C. Mohrmann, "Le latin commun et le latin des chrétiens", in *Études sur le latin des chrétiens*, 3:13–24; see Wilken, "Church's Way of Speaking", and his "The Church as Culture", *First Things* 142 (April 2004): 31–37.

[14] C. Mohrmann, "L'étude de la latinité chrétienne: État de la question, méthodes, résultats", in *Études sur le latin des chrétiens*, 1:83–102.

Tertullian, who wrote in the late second century: "Far less do men agree with our writings, to which no one comes unless he is a Christian already."[15] Even if we take into account Tertullian's usual rhetorical flourish, this passage suggests that the distinctive character of Latin Christian writing in the first three centuries was not just a matter of doctrine, but also a matter of language.[16]

According to Mohrmann, the Peace of the Church in 313 inaugurated a period of humanism in the fourth and fifth centuries, when Christians in their public speaking and writing increasingly used the *spolia gentium*, the "spoils of the Gentiles". This new attitude was made possible by the fact that the Church enjoyed freedom of cult in the Roman Empire and that paganism was no longer seen as an immediate threat. Moreover, the increasing number of converts to the faith from the upper classes of society brought with them a more refined Latinity. The synthesis of these two linguistic strata produced the ecclesiastical Latin of the Middle Ages.[17]

This theory of Christian Latin as a *Sondersprache* was met with reserve by scholars early on.[18] Today, leading students

---

[15] Tertullian, *De testimonio animae* I, 4: CCSL 1:175: "Tanto abest, ut nostris litteris annuant homines, ad quas nemo uenit nisi Christianus."

[16] Cf. A. von Harnack, *The Mission and Expansion of Christianity in the First Three Centuries*, trans. and ed. J. Moffatt, 2 vols., 2nd ed. (London: Williams & Norgate, 1908), 1:370: "In the Latin West, although Minucius Felix and Cyprian (ad Donatum) wrote in a well-bred style, Christian literature had but little to do with the spread of the Christian religion; in the East, upon the contrary, it became a factor of great importance from the third century onwards."

[17] Mohrmann, "Le latin commun et le latin des chrétiens", 24.

[18] See, for instance, J. de Ghellinck, "Latin chrétien ou langue latine des chrétiens?", *Les Études classiques* 8 (1939): 449–78; A. Ferrua, "Latino cristiano antico", *La Civiltà Cattolica* 95 (1944): 35–38, 237–44, and 370–77; S. Cavallini, review of C. Mohrmann, *Latin vulgaire, latin des chrétiens, latin médiéval*, *Gnomon* 29 (1957): 65–69; more recently, R. Coleman, "Vulgar Latin and the

of post-classical Latin, such as Robert Coleman and Philip Burton, are generally critical of the theoretical approach of the Nijmegen school, while its contributions to the study of Latin in late antiquity are still valued. In the first place, historical scholarship has shown that the social background of early converts to Christianity was more varied than suggested by early apologists, such as Minucius Felix, who wrote about the *sermo humilis* used by Christians but did not practice it himself.[19] In fact, the early Christian communities included a number of well-to-do and educated persons from the upper ranks of the Roman Empire. Consequently, the sociological foundations for the *Sondersprache* theory do not hold.[20]

Secondly, the objection is raised that Schrijnen, Mohrmann, and their disciples based their theory on a too restricted selection of sources. Thus Burton notes in his monograph on the Old Latin Gospels that

---

Diversity of Christian Latin", in *Actes du 1er Colloque international sur le latin vulgaire et tardif (Pécs, 2–5 septembre 1985)*, ed. J. Herman (Tübingen, 1987), 37–52, and J.-C. Fredouille, "Latin chrétien ou latin tardif?", *Recherches Augustiniennes* 29 (1996): 5–23. The criticism of E. Rose, "Liturgical Latin in the *Missale Gothicum* (Vat. Reg. Lat. 317): A reconsideration of Christine Mohrmann's approach", *Sacris Erudiri* 42 (2003): 97–121, is not without merit, but overstated.

[19] Minucius Felix, *Octavius* 16: PL 3:280–83. The *Octavius* is not an example of the *sermo humilis* but its opposite: a carefully crafted instance of using the arts of the pagans (in this case, Ciceronian Latin) in the service of Christian apologetics.

[20] Cf. R. Lane Fox, *Pagans and Christians* (London: Viking, 1986), 293–312; P. Brown, *Power and Persuasion in Late Antiquity: Towards a Christian Empire* (Madison: University of Wisconsin Press, 1992), 76; W. Wischmeyer, *Von Golgatha zum Ponte Molle: Studien zur Sozialgeschichte der Kirche im dritten Jahrhundert*, Forschungen zur Kirchen- und Dogmengeschichte 49 (Göttingen: Vandenhoeck & Ruprecht, 1992), 163–203. The superseded view of Christian Latin and its social background is expressed by L. R. Palmer, *The Latin Language* (London: Faber and Faber, 1954), 184: "These two facts are of prime importance for the understanding of Christian Latin: the new religion came in Greek guise and to the simple folk of the back streets."

> the *Sondersprache* theory relies excessively on the evidence of a small number of (mostly) educated writers, that the undoubted peculiarities of Christian Latin do not amount to the system that is claimed, and that Christian writers are often as different in style from one another as they are from their pagan contemporaries.[21]

While acknowledging this critique of the Nijmegen School, it needs to be said that "Christian Latin is no illusion", as Daniel Sheerin says in a recent handbook on medieval Latin.[22] Or, as J.J. O'Donnell writes in his magisterial commentary on Saint Augustine's *Confessions*: "The question of 'Christian Latin' as *Sondersprache* is ripe for fresh and venturesome treatment."[23]

Both Coleman and Burton agree that the uniting feature of the variety of texts that can be subsumed under the heading "Christian Latin" is their *vocabulary*, which distinguishes them from pagan and secular texts. In fact, as Burton comments, "in so far as there was a distinctly Christian idiom, Greek or Latin, its most distinctive component is always likely to have been the language of the Scriptures."[24] This

---

[21] P. Burton, *The Old Latin Gospels: A Study of Their Texts and Language*, Oxford Early Christian Studies (Oxford: Oxford University Press, 2000), 154.

[22] D. Sheerin, "Christian and Biblical Latin", in *Medieval Latin: An Introduction and Bibliographical Guide*, ed. F. A. C. Mantello and A. G. Rigg (Washington, D.C.: Catholic University of America Press, 1996), 150. See also the contribution of S. Deléani, "Les caractères du latin chrétien", in *Il latino e i cristiani: Un bilancio all'inizio del terzo millennio*, ed. E. dal Covolo and M. Sodi, Monumenta Studia Instrumenta Liturgica 17 (Vatican City: Libreria Editrice Vaticana, 2002), 3–25.

[23] O'Donnell, in Augustine, *Confessions*, 1:lxiii.

[24] Burton, *Old Latin Gospels*, 154. Fredouille, "Latin chrétien ou latin tardif?", 17, points toward "un aspect essential de la langue des auteurs chrétiens: leur lexique. Car si ceux-ci ont contribué au renouvellement de la langue latine, c'est, par excellence, dans le domaine du vocabulaire. Cet enrichissement a fait l'objet, depuis plus d'un demi siècle, des travaux de l'École de

is certainly confirmed by Saint Augustine's experience of "the Lord's way of speaking" discussed in the first part of this chapter.[25]

Olegario García de la Fuente identifies biblical Latin as a "special language", which is above all the language of scriptural translations, that is, of books that were originally written in Hebrew (or Aramaic) or in Greek (yet in a Semitic cultural environment). Most of the features that distinguish "Christian Latin" from contemporary use are derived from the Latin of the Sacred Scriptures. According to García de la Fuente, it was the mistake of the Nijmegen school to treat biblical Latin as just one instance of Christian Latin; rather, the whole question needs to be considered from the perspective of the new and in many ways peculiar biblical idiom that entered the Latin cultural sphere.[26]

Robert Coleman rightly insists that any attempt to distinguish characteristics of "Christian Latin" needs to differentiate between the various registers of discourse that existed from early on:

> the vulgarized Latin of Bible and Psalter, the plain but unvulgarized style of ecclesiastical administration, the more sophisticated idiom of expository and hortatory literature and finally

Nimègue, dont l'apport à notre connaissance de la langue des auteurs chrétiens a été considérable, en dépit de certains excès classificatoires contestés."

[25] Cf. also the chapter "Biblical Idioms in the *Confessions*", in P. Burton, *Language in the* Confessions *of Augustine* (Oxford: Oxford University Press, 2007), 212–32.

[26] See the prologue to the second, revised, and enlarged edition of O. García de la Fuente, *Latín bíblico y latín cristiano* (Madrid: Ed. CEES, 1994), 9–10. These reflections emerged from the debate after a lecture the author gave on the subject of his book at the Sorbonne in 1993. For Spanish-language scholarship on the topic, see J. Oroz Reta, ed., *Actas del I Simposio de Latín Cristiano*, Bibliotheca Salmanticensis; Estudios 130 (Salamanca: Univ. Pontificia, 1990) (also published as a volume of the journal *Helmantica* 40 [1989]).

the products of high literary culture—the hymns and collects of the Liturgy and Offices.[27]

Mohrmann, in fact, distinguishes between these different registers in her wide-ranging studies of early Christian texts, and she identifies one particular language, on which, in my view, a fresh treatment of the question of "Christian Latin" could profitably begin: the language of the liturgy. This obviously includes the language of the Scriptures, which are proclaimed in solemn public worship, but also the great variety of prayers and hymns, which are shaped by the Bible in form and content and, at the same time, are monuments of a high literary culture.

This book can in no way claim to venture into a comprehensive treatment of the question; rather, my aim is to indicate essential elements of Latin as a liturgical language that would merit further exploration, and for this purpose it will be necessary to present a brief overview of biblical Latin.

From the Septuagint to the Vetus Latina: At the Origins of Latin Christianity

Initially, Greek was the common language in which the Gospel was preached in the Roman Empire. The cultural and political unity of the Mediterranean world was a providential factor in the spread of the Christian faith, and the diffusion of the Greek language in the urban centers of the empire was a great help in this process. The Greek spoken

[27] Coleman, "Vulgar Latin and the Diversity of Christian Latin", 58. Coleman also notes that these different registers coexisted, in their different functions, "for centuries afterwards, indeed until the vernacularization of the Church's language in our day".

in East and West was not the classical idiom, but the simplified *koinè*, the common language of the various nations living in the eastern part of the Mediterranean world: Greece, Asia Minor, Syria, Palestine, Egypt. *Koinè* Greek was also the language of the urban proletariat in the West that had emigrated there from the eastern territories of the empire. It was the language of uprooted people, prisoners of war, small merchants, sailors, and so on. These people had left their home countries because of wars or for social and economic reasons and flocked into the great cities of the West, above all Rome itself. Rome had become a multi-ethnic city, including a substantial and well-organized Jewish community, which seems to have been mainly Greek speaking. Saint Paul's Letter to the Romans shows that *koinè* was the also the language of the primitive Church in Rome.[28] In fact, Greek continued to be the major language of the Christian community in Rome well into the third century.[29]

The evangelization of the Roman Empire was able to build on a foundation already laid by Hellenistic Jews in the centuries before Christ, that is, the translation of the Hebrew Scriptures into Greek known as the Septuagint. Through the Septuagint, biblical thought was made accessible to the Greek world and language. The religious and cultural importance of this translation project, which has no equal in the ancient world, can hardly be overestimated.[30]

---

[28] Cf. G. Bardy, *La question des langues dans l'Église ancienne*, Études de Théologie Historique (Paris: Beauchesne, 1948), 81–85; W. Meeks, *The First Urban Christians: The Social World of the Apostle Paul* (New Haven: Yale University Press, 1983), 37; see also P. Lampe, *Christians at Rome in the First Two Centuries: From Paul to Valentinus*, trans. M. Steinhauser and ed. M. D. Johnson (London: Continuum, 2006).

[29] Cf. Bardy, *Question des langues*, 81–94.

[30] See A. Léonas, *L'aube des traducteurs: De l'hébreu au grec: Traducteurs et lecteurs de la Bible des Septante IIIe s. av. J.-C.–IVe s. apr. J.-C.*, Initiations

The Septuagint was also an important means of encounter between Christianity and Greco-Roman culture, as noted by Pope Benedict XVI in his Regensburg speech of September 12, 2006:

> Today we know that the Greek translation of the Old Testament produced at Alexandria—the Septuagint—is more than a simple (and in that sense really less than satisfactory) translation of the Hebrew text: it is an independent textual witness and a distinct and important step in the history of revelation, one which brought about this encounter in a way that was decisive for the birth and spread of Christianity.[31]

To a Greek reader in antiquity, the language of the Septuagint was conspicuous for its many "barbaric" words. These were not only the Hebrew names of persons and places (Moses, David, Sion, Samaria, and so on), but also the transliterations of certain unfamiliar terms like "manna" (μάν in Ex 16:31 and elsewhere) or "teraphim" for household idols (θεϱαφιν in Judges 18:4 and 1 Samuel 15:23). The alienating effect of this unusual vocabulary should not be underestimated, and early Christian theologians, such as Origen, John Chrysostom, Isidor of Pelusium, and Theodoret of Cyrus, felt it necessary to defend the Greek Bible against the criticism of their educated contemporaries.[32] Theodoret responds

---

bibliques (Paris: Cerf, 2007), 33–40, esp. 33, where he notes: "Le fait que la Bible grecque des Septante soit la première traduction au sens moderne du terme fait au sein de la tradition culturelle occidentale, est largement reconnu aujourd'hui."

[31] Benedict XVI, *Faith, Reason and the University: Memories and Reflections: Lecture at the Meeting with the Representatives of Science in the Aula Magna of the University of Regensburg* (September 12, 2006).

[32] Cf. Léonas, *Aube des traducteurs*, 126–32: "Le mot barbares"; and Léonas, *Recherches sur le langage de la Septante*, Orbis Biblicus et Orientalis

that, for Christians, there is nothing exotic in these names; on the contrary, they know them as well as those of their own children.[33]

Moreover, as Alexis Léonas argues in his work on the language of the Septuagint, there are other unusual linguistic elements in biblical Greek that helped to create a "sacred style" or "hieratic register". Léonas shows that these stylistic particularities were already noted as such by readers in late antiquity, as is evident from the philological notes of Hadrian's *Introduction to the Holy Scriptures* (early fifth century).[34] To mention only a few examples:

—Among the lexicological elements, there is the metaphorical use of certain expressions that convey essential theological ideas, such as "chalice" (ποτήριον) for chastisement (Ps 10:6, Is 51:22 et al.), "betrothal" (μνηστεία) for covenant with God (Hos 2:19, 21), or "adultery" (μοιχεία) for idolatry (Is 50:1, Jer 3:8).

—Moreover, there are specific usages, such as that of οὐρανός in the plural ("the heavens", for example, Ps 148:1).

—The Septuagint often adopts a syntax and word order that is uncommon in classical Greek, as in Psalm 31[32]:32–4: "Because (ὅτι) I was silent my bones grew old; whilst I cried out all the day long. / Because (ὅτι) for day and night thy hand was heavy upon me: I am

211 (Fribourg: Academic Press; Göttingen: Vandenhoeck & Ruprecht, 2005), 104–9.

[33] See, for instance, Theodoret of Cyrus, *Graecorum affectionum curatio* V, 64: SC 57:247.

[34] F. Goessling, *Adrians* ΕΙΣΑΓΩΓΗ ΕΙΣ ΤΑΣ ΘΕΙΑΣ ΓΡΑΦΑΣ *aus neu aufgefundenen Handschriften herausgegeben, übersetzt und erläutert* (Berlin: Reuther, 1887). See Léonas, *Recherches sur le langage de la Septante*, 148–228, with many examples.

turned in my anguish, whilst the thorn is fastened" (Douai-Rheims version, modified).

—Peculiarities in syntax and word order often coincide with the use of rhetorical figures, such as antistrophe, that is, the repetition of the same word or phrase at the beginning of every clause, as in Psalm 88[89]:10–11: "Thou (σὺ) dost rule the raging of the sea; when its waves rise, thou stillest them. / Thou (σὺ) didst crush Rahab like a carcass, thou didst scatter thy enemies with thy mighty arm."

—The Septuagint faithfully reproduces another typical element of Hebrew biblical poetry, the *parallelismus membrorum*, for example, in Amos 5:24: "But let justice roll down like waters, and righteousness like an ever-flowing stream" (synonymous parallelism), or Proverbs 10:1: "A wise son makes a glad father, but a foolish son is a sorrow to his mother" (antithetical parallelism).[35]

Many, though by no means all, of these features of a "hieratic register" are taken from the poetic parts of the Hebrew Bible, especially the Psalms. This is significant, because the Psalter was later to become the "prayer book" of the Church and contributed much to the development of liturgical language.

Thanks to the language of the Septuagint, which also shaped the writings of the New Testament books, Greek-speaking Christians already had a linguistic medium through

[35] The characteristic parallelisms of Hebrew poetry are occasionally found in the letters of Saint Paul (for example, 1 Corinthians 13:1–3) and, above all, in the New Testament canticles; cf. E. Norden, *Die antike Kunstprosa vom VI. Jahrhundert v. Chr. bis in die Zeit der Renaissance*, 2 vols., 2nd ed. (Leipzig: Teubner, 1909), 2:509–10, and C. Mohrmann, *Liturgical Latin: Its Origins and Character: Three Lectures* (London: Burns & Oates, 1959), 16–17.

which they could express and communicate their new faith. Latin-speaking Christians had to make a greater effort in this regard, because they could not rely on an already established biblical idiom in their mother tongue. As Christianity was spreading in the western part of the Roman Empire, it soon became necessary to translate the Holy Scriptures for those who were not able to understand the Greek of the Septuagint or of the New Testament. The earliest Latin Bible versions were *ad hoc* translations for the use of individual Christian communities and are usually referred to by the collective name *Vetus Latina*. There was a great variety of translations, and they were of a mixed quality, as both Jerome and Augustine observed. The latter laments in his *De doctrina christiana* that "in the early days of the faith, any person who got hold of a Greek manuscript and fancied that he had some ability in the two languages went ahead and translated it." [36]

From a linguistic perspective, the *Vetus Latina* translations are commonly described as "vulgar" and "literal". This is certainly correct, if we take "Vulgar Latin", with Jószef Herman and Roger Wright, as "just a collective label, available for use to refer to all those features of the Latin language that are known to have existed, from textual attestations and incontrovertible reconstructions, but that were not recommended by the grammarians".[37] From the perspective of classical Latin grammar, the *Vetus Latina* texts are full of "vulgarisms", that is, non-standard usages, which Robert

[36] Augustine, *De doctrina christiana* II, 36 (ix, 16), ed. and trans. R. P. H. Green (Oxford: Clarendon Press, 1995), 73. See Jerome, *Praefatio ad Damasum*, in *Biblia sacra iuxta Vulgatam versionem*, ed. R. Weber and R. Gryson, 4th ed. (Stuttgart: Deutsche Bibelgesellschaft, 1994), 1515–16.

[37] R. Wright, "Foreword", in J. Herman, *Vulgar Latin*, trans. R. Wright (University Park, Pa.: Pennsylvania State University Press, 2000), ix.

Coleman notes in various Old Latin manuscripts of Matthew 13:1–3: for instance, the use of the preposition *in* with the temporal ablative and of *dies* as feminine (*in illa die*), the use of *secus* for the classical *iuxta*, *populus* for *turba*, and so on.[38]

The question of the many literalisms in the *Vetus Latina* is more complicated, as Coleman notes, since their presence may indicate either "a Greek-speaking translator's imperfect command of Latin or . . . a determination to preserve as closely as possible the linguistic form of the sacred text".[39] Burton concludes from his detailed study of the *Vetus Latina* Gospels that their "literal" character is the result of a consciously adopted translation technique. The translators intended to achieve an exact correspondence between source language and target language, thereby taking into account distortions of natural use and idiom.[40] This is not at all unexpected, for, according to Sebastian Brock, in biblical translation, a word-for-word approach was usually preferred. A sense-for-sense approach would presuppose that the translator is able to comprehend the full sense of the original, and this would contradict the belief in the infinite riches of the Bible,[41] which is epitomized in Jerome's saying that in Holy Scripture "even the word order is a mystery."[42]

---

[38] See Coleman, "Vulgar Latin and the Diversity of Christian Latin", 39–40.

[39] Ibid., 40.

[40] See Burton, *Old Latin Gospels*, 87–95.

[41] S. P. Brock, "Aspects of Translation Technique in Antiquity", *Greek, Roman and Byzantine Studies* 20 (1979) (= *Syriac Perspectives on Late Antiquity*, Collected Studies Series 199 [London: Variorum Reprints, 1984], no. III), 70–79.

[42] Jerome, *Ep.* 57, 5: CSEL 54:508: "Ego enim non solum fateor, sed libera uoce profiteor me in interpretatione Graecorum absque scripturis sanctis, ubi et uerborum ordo mysterium est, non uerbum e uerbo sed sensum exprimere de sensu."

The *Vetus Latina* translations are obviously influenced by the language of the Greek source in their morphology and lexis. For the sake of brevity, I shall limit the discussion here to two phenomena: calques and loanwords.

Calques

According to a standard definition, calquing or loan-translation "consists in translating morphologically complex foreign expressions by means of novel combinations of native elements which match the meaning and structure of the foreign expressions and their component parts".[43] In the *Vetus Latina* Gospels, there are various examples of neologisms that match exactly the structure of the Greek:

—*beneplacere/beneplacitum* for εὐδοκέω/εὐδοκία;

—*glorificare*, *clarificare* for δοξάζω;

—*sanctificare* for ἁγιάζω.[44]

Loanwords

The *Vetus Latina* is characterized by its many loanwords, some of which are commonly used in various spheres of life (travel, trade, food, clothing, measures, administration,

[43] See H. Hock, *Principles of Historical Linguistics* (Berlin, New York, and Amsterdam: Mouton de Gruyter, 1988), 388.

[44] For further examples, also of the related phenomena of the use of established words that match exactly the morphological structure of the original (for example, *immundus* for ἀκαθαρτός and *regulus* for ὁ βασιλικός) and of the revival of old-fashioned formations that match the original (for example, *benedicere* = εὐλογέω), see Burton, *Old Latin Gospels*, 129–36.

and so on); their presence in "vulgar" Latin texts is not worthy of particular note.[45]

Of another category is the particularly Jewish and Christian vocabulary, which came from Semitic languages through Greek (including proper Jewish nouns and titles), such as *alleluia, amen, azyma, osanna, sabbatum,* or was inherited from the early, Greek period of Western Christianity, such as *apostolus, baptisma/-us, charisma, diaconus, episcopus, evangelium, martyr.*

Some of these words had already acquired a "sacred" association so that they were preferred even when another Latin term was available, such as *baptisma/-us* for *(in)tinctio* or *lavacrum* and *baptizo* for *(in)inting(u)o* or *lavo.*[46]

Burton also notes that the translators of the *Vetus Latina* Gospels seem to have been intent on finding "precisely the right word irrespective of antiquity, and . . . precisely the right set phrase".[47] This search for the *mot juste* may be illustrated by two examples taken from Burton:[48]

—*diluculo* for πρωὶ ἔννυχα λίαν in Mark 1:35. The word had a classical pedigree, but its exact meaning was no longer widely known. The *Vetus Latina* uses *diluculum* in a very precise way, indicating the early morning around the time of sunrise;[49] later the word became

[45] Cf. ibid., 137–41; Herman, *Vulgar Latin,* 105–7.

[46] Cf. Burton, *Old Latin Gospels,* 144–45. The alternative terms rarely appear in Latin Christian authors, among them Tertullian and Cyprian.

[47] Ibid., 103.

[48] See ibid., 106–7.

[49] See Gregory the Great, *Moralia in Iob* VIII, xxix, 48: CCSL 143:419: "Diluculum dicitur, cum iam nocturna tempora in claritatem lucis mutantur." Cf. S. Bäumer, *Geschichte des Breviers: Versuch einer quellenmäßigen Darstellung der Entwicklung des altkirchlichen und des römischen Officiums bis auf unsere Tage* (Freiburg im Breisgau: Herder, 1895; repr., Bonn: nova & vetera, 2004), 19–20.

current in the Vulgate as well as in other Christian Latin texts.

—*baiulare* for βαστάζω in some *Vetus Latina* versions of Luke 14:27 (*qui non baiulat crucem suam*) and John 19:17 (*et baiulans sibi crucem*). Although the word is mainly found in Roman comedy, this does not mean that it is "vulgar". In the Gospels it is employed in a very precise way: carrying the cross by placing one's weight under the burden, as opposed to carrying it in one's arms.

Similarly, the syntax of the *Vetus Latina* shows many nonclassical constructions and often follows the Hebrew or Greek source so closely that the Latin idiom is bent.[50] However, as Burton notes for the Gospel versions, the characterization of their syntax as "literal" and "vulgar" needs to be qualified, because similar phenomena to those in morphology and syntax can be observed here as well: there are cases where the translators occasionally retrieve some obsolete classical use, and there are also cases where they choose among several options the Latin construction that is most fitting in the given context. Both phenomena would certainly seem to indicate a native speaker's command of the Latin language.[51] It is worth noting here that Jerome not infrequently adopts a more literal translation of the Greek in the Vulgate Gospels than what is found in their Old Latin predecessors.[52]

---

[50] Cf. the list of Sheerin, "Christian and Biblical Latin", 146–48.

[51] Cf. Burton, *Old Latin Gospels*, 172–91. See also G. Rubio, "Semitic Influence in the History of Latin Syntax", in *New Perspectives on Historical Latin Syntax*, ed. P. Bald and P. Cuzzolin, vol. 1, Trends in Linguistics: Studies & Monographs 180.1 (Berlin and New York, 2009), 195–239.

[52] See Burton, *Old Latin Gospels*, 192–99. On Jerome's translation technique, see also C. Rico, "L'art de la traduction chez Saint Jérôme: La Vulgate

New Wine into New Wineskins

This brief and necessarily generalized overview of the linguistic characteristics of the Old Latin Bible versions would seem to allow the following conclusion: However their literary quality was judged from the classical point of view, they were extremely important for expressing the Christian faith in the Latin language. In particular, the many neologisms of the *Vetus Latina*, which then became stock Christian vocabulary, far from being simply an indication of "vulgar" Latin, are a powerful testimony to the early Church's awareness of the newness of God's revelation in Christ. To use a biblical image: the new wine of the Gospel had to be poured into new wineskins (Mt 9:17; Mk 2:22; Lk 5:37–39).

Burton reminds us in his study of the *Vetus Latina* Gospels that "the mere presence of alien usages in the Latin may actually enhance the prestige of the translation among the Christian community, by reinforcing a sense of community apart from the world."[53] This may partially account for the fact that Latin-speaking Christians were more reticent than their Greek-speaking coreligionists in the process of receiving the heritage of classical culture. The East was in general more susceptible to classical *paideia* than the West, as Edward Watts argues in his recent study *City and School in Late Antique Athens and Alexandria.*[54] Various factors contributed to this, for instance, the fact that Greek was further developed than

à l'aune de la Néovulgate: L'exemple du quatrième évangile", *Revue des Études Latines* 83 (2006): 194–218, and "La traduction du sens littéral chez saint Jérôme", in *Le sens littéral des Écritures*, ed. O.-T. Venard, Collection Lectio Divina, Hors Série (Paris: Cerf, 2009), 171–218.

[53] Burton, *Old Latin Gospels*, 28.

[54] See E.J. Watts, *City and School in Late Antique Athens and Alexandria*, The Transformation of the Classical Heritage 41 (Berkeley: University of California Press, 2006), 14–21. At the same time, Watts notes that "for every

Latin as a medium for expressing abstract thought. Thus Cicero in particular complained about the poverty of philosophical vocabulary in Latin.[55] A major factor would certainly seem to be the different linguistic attitudes in the Greek East and in the Latin West, as Mohrmann has argued:

> Early on the East sought to establish a closer tie with the classical Greek heritage, and did not hesitate to use the old, Greek words with a new Christian meaning. The West, though not rejecting this proceeding, sought, in this respect too, a greater and more complete isolation. The West was also more conservative. More than the East, it jealously guarded its old, biblically inspired, linguistic patrimony.[56]

Greek Christian authors were quite happy to take an already existing word from the classical tradition and invest it with a new meaning. Latin Christian authors, by contrast, tended to form a completely new word or else used a Greek (or Hebrew) loanword, being particularly keen to avoid any association with pagan ideas. The difference between these two attitudes can be illustrated with the help of a significant example: when speaking of Jesus as "Savior", Greek Christians used the already existing σωτήϱ, despite its pagan pedigree. The word occurs in Pindar and Aeschylus as a title given to Greek deities, among them Zeus, Athena, and especially Asclepius, the god of healing. In the Hellenistic world, rulers were acclaimed as σωτήϱ if they had liberated a city from oppression, siege, or a similar threat.

Jerome there was a Sidonius Apollinaris who eagerly embraced both Christianity and classical culture": ibid., 15.

[55] For example, Cicero, *De finibus* 1; see T. Fögen, *Patrii sermonis egestas: Einstellungen lateinischer Autoren zu ihrer Muttersprache*, Beiträge zur Altertumskunde 150 (Munich and Leipzig: K. G. Saur, 2000), passim.

[56] Mohrmann, "Linguistic Problems in the Early Christian Church", *Études sur le latin des chrétiens* 3:196.

Despite this pagan use, σωτήρ found its way into the Septuagint, where God is invoked as "Savior" (for example, Ps 24:5; 26:9; Mic 7:7). In the New Testament, it has a specifically Christological meaning and refers to Jesus the Savior (Lk 2:11; Acts 13:23; Phil 3:20, and so on).

Latin speakers found it difficult to render this term in their own language, even in classical times. Cicero was already looking for an appropriate Latin word and declared that he could not find one; he used *salus*, *parens (ac deus) salutis*, *servator*, and *salutaris* or chose periphrastic expressions, such as *qui salutem dedit*.[57] Propertius and Livy employed the word *servator*, while Tacitus preferred *conservator*. These renderings were not accepted in Christian popular speech, let alone in theological writing, most likely because of their pagan religious overtones; however, *conservator* is later found in Christian poetry, often for the sake of the meter. Tertullian's invention, *salutificator*, did not have any success, nor had Arnobius' choice, *sospitator*. After attempts at translating σωτήρ with *salutaris*, which was also used as an epithet of the god Jupiter, Latin-speaking Christians coined the neologism *salvator*. *Salvator* became a current term only by the late fourth century, and even then Christian authors showed some reserve toward it. Augustine, in his treatise *De fide et symbolo*, dating from the year 392, uses the term *reparator*, a word with a pagan connotation.[58] It obviously took a while for the educated rhetorician to accept the Christian

[57] Cicero, *In Verrem* II, 2, 154: "Itaque cum non solum patronum illius insulae, sed etiam SOTERA inscriptum vidi Syracusis. Hoc quantum est? Ita magnum ut Latine uno verbo exprimi non possit. Is est nimirum SOTER qui salutem dedit"; see P. Labriolle, "Salvator", *Archivum Latinitatis Mediae Aetatis* 14 (1939): 26–28, with further references, and C. Mohrmann, "Les emprunts grecs dans la latinité chrétienne", in *Études sur le latin des chrétiens*, 3:131–39.

[58] Augustine, *De fide et symbolo* IV, 6: CSEL 41:9.

neologism. He might have remembered advice similar to that of Julius Caesar, as transmitted by Aulus Gellius: "Avoid a strange and unfamiliar word as you would a dangerous reef." [59] In one of his later sermons, Augustine explains the expression "Christ Jesus", which is so often found in the letters of the Apostle Paul, as follows:

> "Christ Jesus", he says, that is, "Christ the Savior" [*salvator*]. For this is Jesus in Latin. Let not grammarians seek for what is proper Latin, but let Christians seek for what is true. For *salus* is a Latin word. *Salvare* and *salvator* were not Latin [words] until the Savior [*salvator*] came; when he came to the Latins, he made those [words] Latin, too.[60]

By then, Augustine had obviously made his peace with biblical neologisms, but it is worth noting that he still feels the need to explain them; he gives a similar explanation in book 13 of his *De Trinitate*.[61]

Latin Christian authors, like their Greek counterparts, had to defend the language of the Holy Scriptures against criticism from educated pagans. A common approach was to argue that the "simple style" of the Bible was intended, because it helped the universal spread of the Christian message. However, later Church Fathers attempted to find a

[59] Aulus Gellius, *Noctes Atticae* I, 10, 4: "Habe semper in memoria atque in pectore, ut tanquam scopulum sic fugias inauditum atque insolens verbum."

[60] Augustine, *Sermo* 299, 6: PL 38:1371: "Christus inquit Jesus, id est Christus salvator, Hoc est enim latine Jesus. Nec quaerant grammatici quam sit latinum, sed christiani quam verum. Salus enim latinum nomen est. Salvare et Salvator non fuerunt haec latina antequam veniret Salvator: quando ad latinos venit, et haec latina fecit."

[61] Augustine, *De Trinitate* XIII, x, 14: CCSL 50A:401: "Qui est hebraice Iesus, graece σωτήρ, nostra autem locutione saluator. Quod uerbum latina lingua antea non habebat, sed habere poterat sicut potuit quando voluit." Cf. Mohrmann, "Comment saint Augustin s'est familiarisé", 387.

new appreciation of the Scripture's literary form. Jerome somewhat apologetically conceded the *novitas* of biblical Latin, which is evident in its borrowings from Greek and from Hebrew, but then pointed toward the philosophical writings of Cicero, who borrowed many expressions from Greek.[62] Ambrose argued that the Bible was written, not according to received aesthetic and rhetorical forms (*secundum artem*), but according to the superior grace of inspiration (*secundum gratiam quae super omnem artem est*).[63] Likewise, Augustine saw a proper kind of eloquence (*eloquentia*) in the divinely inspired writings.[64]

---

[62] Jerome, *In ep. ad Gal.* 1 (ad 1, 12): PL 26:328.

[63] Ambrose, *Ep.* 55, 1: CSEL 82/2:77; cf. A. Kamesar, "Ambrose, Philo and the Presence of Art in the Bible", *Journal of Early Christian Studies* 9 (2001): 73–103, esp. 73–75.

[64] Augustine, *De doctrina christiana* IV, 25 (vi, 9) and 31 (vii, 11): ed. Green, 206 and 208. On the question of the "sermo humilis", see the still valuable contribution of E. Auerbach, *Literatursprache und Publikum in der lateinischen Spätantike und im Mittelalter* (Bern: Francke, 1958), 25–63.

II

SACRED LANGUAGE

Genuine poetry can communicate before it is understood.

— T. S. Eliot[1]

The previous chapter has touched upon certain elements of syntax and vocabulary in biblical Greek and biblical Latin that helped to create a "hieratic" or "sacred" style. The idea of a "sacred language" is essential for understanding liturgical language, especially (though not exclusively) in the Latin tradition. In order to approach this subject, we need to recall that languages exist, not in a vacuum, but in the context of a structured system that is determined by a variety of factors (social, cultural, psychological, and so on). The language used in the Church's solemn public worship has obviously developed under certain specific conditions and circumstances that need to be considered to understand its particular characteristics.

It will be expedient to follow the argument of Christine Mohrmann, which is based on the theory developed by Ferdinand de Saussure and other exponents of the Geneva school

---

[1] T. S. Eliot, "Dante", in *Selected Prose of T. S. Eliot*, ed. F. Kermode (London: Faber and Faber, 1975), 205.

of linguistics, that language should be seen not only as a means of social communication in ordinary life, but also as a medium of expression of persons in a comprehensive sense. Human speech is not just a utilitarian instrument that serves to communicate facts and should do so in the most simple and efficient manner; it also provides the forms of expressing and interpreting the rich and subtle workings of the human mind, including the arts, philosophy, and religion.[2]

Language is also the medium in which we express religious thoughts and experiences. We are conscious of the transcendence of the divine and, at the same time, of its presence—a presence that is both real and incomprehensible. There are extreme forms of expressing this experience: "speaking in tongues" and "mystical silence". Speaking in tongues, or *glossolalia*, is a phenomenon familiar to us from Saint Paul's First Letter to the Corinthians and has had an astonishing revival in the last hundred years in the charismatic movements; it also known in other religious traditions, for example, the Oracle of Delphi. *Glossolalia* makes human communication impossible; the person who speaks "in tongues" can be understood only with the help of an interpreter. Saint Paul clearly has reservations about *glossolalia* and prefers "prophecy", because this is in the service of charity and builds up the Church (1 Cor 14). In "mystical silence", human communication is excluded as well, as in the Apostle's experience of "being caught up to the third heaven", when he "heard things that cannot be told, which man may not utter" (2 Cor 12:2–4).

"Sacred language" does not go as far as *glossolalia* and mystical silence in excluding human communication

[2] Thus C. Mohrmann, *Liturgical Latin: Its Origins and Character: Three Lectures* (London: Burns & Oates, 1959), 1–26.

completely, or at least in attempting to do so. However, it reduces the element of comprehensibility in favor of other elements, notably that of expression. Mohrmann proposes to see in sacred language, and in particular in its vocabulary, a specific way of organizing religious experience. She also argues that every form of belief in the supernatural, in the existence of a transcendent being, leads necessarily to adopting a form of sacred language in worship—just as a consistent secularism leads to rejecting any form of it.

Sacred language is the medium of expression, not just of individuals, but of a community living according to certain traditions. Its linguistic forms are handed down from generation to generation; they are often deliberately "stylized" and removed from contemporary language. There exists a similar phenomenon in the field of literature, *Homerische Kunstsprache*, the stylized language of the Homeric epos with its consciously archaic and colorful word forms. The language of the *Iliad* and the *Odyssey*, which is also found in Hesiod and in later poetic inscriptions, was never a spoken language used in everyday life.[3]

With Mohrmann, we can name three characteristics of sacred or, as she also says, "hieratic" language:

1. Sacred language is stable; it shows tenacity in holding on to archaic linguistic forms. In the pagan Roman tradition, this characteristic was so pronounced that for centuries prayers were used when their meaning was not even understood by the priests who recited them. A similar phenomenon seems to have arisen in the early Middle Ages, when command of Latin had become so poor that prayer

[3] See ibid., 10–11. Cf. the seminal work by K. Meister, *Die homerische Kunstsprache*, Preisschriften der Fürstlich-Jablonowskischen Gesellschaft 48 (Leipzig: Teubner, 1921).

texts were transmitted in a form that made them hardly intelligible and distorted their sense (more on this in chapter 4 below).

2. Foreign elements are introduced in order to associate with ancient religious tradition; a case in point is the Hebrew biblical vocabulary in the Latin use of Christians. Augustine makes pertinent observations on this in his *De doctrina christiana*: "In some cases, although they could be translated, the original form is preserved for the sake of its solemn authority [*propter sanctiorem auctoritatem*]", such as *amen* and *alleluia*. Other words "are said to be incapable of being translated into another language. . . . This is especially true of interjections, which signify emotion, rather than an element of clearly conceived meaning"; as examples he provides *osanna* and *raca*, the expression of anger mentioned in Matthew 5:22.[4]

3. Sacred language uses rhetorical figures that are typical of oral style, such as parallelism and antithesis, rhythmic clausulae, rhyme, and alliteration.[5]

It should be noted that by "sacred language" I do not mean to refer here to the medieval tradition of Hebrew,

---

[4] Augustine, *De doctrina christiana* II, 34–35 (xi, 16): ed. and trans. R. P. H. Green, Oxford Early Christian Texts (Oxford: Clarendon Press, 1995), 73. On the meaning of *os(i)anna*, there is an interesting exchange of letters between Pope Damasus and Jerome: *Ep. 19–20*: CSEL 54:103–10. The correspondence with Damasus was most likely revised by Jerome for the purpose of publication: cf. U. Reutter, *Damasus, Bischof von Rom (366–384): Leben und Werk*, Studien und Texte zu Antike und Christentum 55 (Tübingen: Mohr Siebeck, 2009), 23–30.

[5] See C. Mohrmann, "The Ever-Recurring Problem of Language in the Church", in *Études sur le latin des chrétiens*, 4 vols., Storia e letteratura 65, 87, 103, 143 (Rome: Edizioni di Storia e Letteratura, 1961–1977), 4:151–52.

Greek, and Latin as the *tres linguae sacrae* of Christianity. Church Fathers, such as Hilary of Poitiers and Augustine of Hippo, already honored the three languages that were used on the title of Christ's Cross according to John 19:20, because they had a special significance in the history of salvation and the preaching of the Gospel. Thus Hilary attributed particular merit to Hebrew, Greek, and Latin, not because of some inherent quality, but because in these languages "is preached above all the mystery of the will of God and the expectation of the coming Kingdom of God".[6] Likewise, Augustine commented on the title of the Cross: "These three languages were prominent there before all others: Hebrew on behalf of the Jews who boasted in the law of God; Greek on behalf of the wise men among the pagans; Latin on behalf of the Romans who at that time were dominating many and almost all peoples."[7] This patristic reading entered medieval exegesis, and Augustine's commentary in particular was regularly quoted by later theologians.

It would appear that no author actually called these three languages "sacred" before Isidore of Seville (ca. 560–636).[8] He considered Hebrew, Greek, and Latin sacred because they were the languages of Sacred Scripture and insisted that familiarity with them was necessary for correct exegesis. There is no reference, however, whether explicit or implicit, to the Church's liturgy in Isidore. Later Latin authors reflected on the use of the three sacred languages of Scripture in divine worship, but this discussion always remained within the Latin rites, whether Gallican or Roman (see below in chapter 5, pp. 143–45). This idea of the *tres linguae sacrae*,

[6] Hilary of Poitiers, *Tractatus super psalmos, prol.* 15: CSEL 22:13.

[7] Augustine of Hippo, *In Joan. Ev. tract.* 117, 4: CCSL 36:653.

[8] Isidore of Seville, *Etymologiae* IX, 1, 3–4: PL 82:326: "Tres autem sunt linguae sacrae...."

which was widely received in the Middle Ages, is manifestly different from the doctrine that has become known as "trilinguism", according to which the liturgy could be celebrated only in Hebrew, Greek, and Latin. While it is often said that this view was common among the Franks who opposed the missionary work of Saint Cyril and Saint Methodius,[9] Francis J. Thomson has shown that "trilinguism" was rather a generic piece of Byzantine polemics against the Latin West. As he concludes from his comprehensive study of the available material, "the notion that the Western Church ever propagated trilinguism in the Cyrillo-Methodian sense belongs to the realm of myth, not history."[10]

Early Eucharistic Prayers

The aforementioned characteristics of sacred language emerge clearly from the early history of the Eucharistic Prayers. It is generally agreed that these were relatively fluid in the first three centuries. Their exact wording was not yet fixed, and the celebrant had some room to improvise. However, as Allan Bouley notes, "Conventions governing the structure and content of improvised anaphoras are ascertainable in the second century and indicate that extempore prayer

[9] See, for instance, K. Pecklers, *Dynamic Equivalence: The Living Language of Christian Worship* (Collegeville: Liturgical Press, 2003), 4–7.

[10] F.J. Thomson, "SS. Cyril and Methodius and a Mythical Western Heresy: Trilinguism: A Contribution to the Study of Patristic and Mediaeval Theories of Sacred Languages", *Analecta Bollandiana* 110 (1992): 96; cf. T.M. Kolbaba, *The Byzantine Lists: Errors of the Latins*, Illinois Medieval Studies (Chicago: University of Illinois Press, 2000), 66–67. Thomson, 75, argues that "Western opposition to Cyril and Methodius' innovations was not so much directed against the use of Slavonic as against the invention of an entirely new alphabet."

was not left merely to the whim of the minister. In the third century, and possibly even before, some anaphoral texts already existed in writing." Bouley speaks of an "atmosphere of controlled freedom",[11] because concerns for orthodoxy limited the celebrant's liberty to vary the texts of the prayer. This need became particularly pressing during the doctrinal struggles of the fourth century; hence this era saw the emergence of fixed Eucharistic Prayers, such as the Roman Canon, the Anaphora of Saint John Chrysostom, and others.

There is another important aspect of this development: the freedom to improvise existed only within a framework of fixed elements of content and style, which was, above all, biblically inspired. In a recent study on improvisation in prayer, Achim Budde analyzes three oriental Anaphoras used over a considerable geographical area: the Egyptian version of the Anaphora of Saint Basil, the West Syrian Anaphora of Saint James, and the East Syrian Anaphora of Nestorius. With his comparative method, the German liturgist identifies common features of structure, style, and rhetoric. Budde argues that these patterns and stable elements go back to the pre-literary history of these Eucharistic Prayers and that they were studied and even memorized by priests in the early Church.[12] As noted by the Norwegian exegete Sigmund

[11] A. Bouley, *From Freedom to Formula: The Evolution of the Eucharistic Prayer from Oral Improvisation to Written Texts*, Studies in Christian Antiquity 21 (Washington, D.C.: Catholic University of America Press, 1981), xv; on the emergence of fixed forms in Eucharistic Prayers, see also A. Gelston, *The Eucharistic Prayer of Addai and Mari* (Oxford: Clarendon Press, 1992), 11–21.

[12] A. Budde, "Improvisation im Eucharistiegebet: Zur Technik freien Betens in der Alten Kirche", *Jahrbuch für Antike und Christentum* 44 (2001): 127–44, esp. 138, where he concludes that "die Stabilität solcher noch heute am Text erkennbarer Schemata ein Hinweis darauf, dass sie gezielt auswendig gelernt

Mowinckel, known especially for his work on the Psalms, rapid development of fixed forms of prayer corresponds to an essential religious need and constitutes a fundamental law of religion.[13] Budde's methodological approach is an important supplement and corrective to that of Bouley, who would appear to underestimate the significance of memorization in an oral culture.[14] The formation of stable liturgical texts can thus be ascertained from early on as a strong force in the process of handing on the Christian faith.

In the Western tradition, the freedom to improvise remained for a longer time than in the East, especially in certain liturgical prayers, such as the introductory part of the Eucharistic Prayer we now call "Preface".[15] This is the reason why there is such a great variety of Prefaces in the

---

und eingeübt wurden." See also J. Hammerstaedt and P. Terbuyken, "Improvisation", *Reallexikon für Antike und Christentum* 17 (1996): 1212–84.

[13] S. Mowinckel, *Religion und Kultus*, trans. A. Schauer (Göttingen: Vandenhoeck & Ruprecht, 1953), 8: "Aber die festen Formen entwickeln sich sehr schnell. Und das braucht in keiner Weise ein Verfallszeichen, eine 'Erstarrung' zu sein, sondern entspricht in Wirklichkeit einem primären religiösen Bedürfnis, einem Grundgesetz der Religion"; cf. ibid., 14 and 53.

[14] Cf. Budde, "Improvisation im Eucharistiegebet", 137: "Nun ist die Feier der Eucharistie der breiteste Strom christlicher Überlieferung überhaupt: ein Ritus, der bald in jeder Gemeinde jede Woche vollzogen wird. Aus beinahe innerer Notwendigkeit stellen sich dabei Verfestigungen ein. . . . Die liturgievergleichende Forschung hat diesem Modus der Überlieferung und seiner Kraft zur Stabilisierung des konkreten Wortlautes bislang viel zu wenig zugetraut und jede Häufung wörtlicher Parallelen allein durch redaktionelle Vorgänge zu erklären versucht. Tatsächlich aber müssen auch umfangreiche wörtliche Übereinstimmungen nicht zwangsläufig auf literarische Verwandtschaft hinweisen. Denn die Verfestigung der euchologischen Gepflogenheiten befindet sich längst in einem fortgeschrittenen Stadium, als die Protagonisten des 4. Jahrhunderts das 'vorgeschriebene' Formular erfinden."

[15] Cf. B. Botte and C. Mohrmann, *L'ordinaire de la messe: Texte critique, traduction et études*, Études liturgique 2 (Paris: Cerf; Louvain: Abbaye du Mont César, 1953), 39–40, and C. Mohrmann, "Sur l'histoire de Praefari-Praefatio", in *Études sur le latin des chrétiens*, 3:291–305.

early Roman sacramentaries. Mohrmann concludes that it is "this system which leads to a marked traditional prayer style".[16] A similar phenomenon can be observed in the earliest Greek epos: the freedom of individual singers to improvise on the given material led to a stylized language. In the liturgy, the early tradition of oral improvisation in prayer helped to create a sacred style.

Mohrmann introduces a useful distinction between sacred languages of a "primary" and a "secondary" kind. "Primary" sacred languages were formed as such from the beginning, for example, the language of the Greek oracles that was close to the *Kunstsprache* of the Homeric epos. "Secondary" sacred languages have come to be experienced as such only in the course of time. The languages used in Christian worship would seem to fall under this category: Greek in the Byzantine tradition; Syriac in the Patriarchate of Antioch and the "Nestorian" Church of the East, with its missions reaching to India and China; Old Armenian; Old Georgian; Coptic; Old Ethiopian (*Ge'ez*); Church Slavonic; not to forget the Elizabethan English of the *Book of Common Prayer*[17] and the German used in the Lutheran books of worship (from the *Brandenburgisch-Nürnbergische Kirchenordnung* of 1533 to the *Lutherische Agende I* of 1955);[18]

---

[16] Mohrmann, *Liturgical Latin*, 24.

[17] Cf. F.E. Brightman, *The English Rite: Being a Synopsis of the Sources and Revisions of the Book of Common Prayer with an Introduction and an Appendix*, 2 vols., 2nd ed. (1921; repr., Farnborough: Gregg International, 1970).

[18] Cf. H. Westermayer, *Die Brandenburgisch-Nürnbergische Kirchenvisitation und Kirchenordnung 1528–1533: Auf Grund der Akten dargestellt* (Erlangen: Junge, 1894), and *Agende für evangelisch-lutherische Kirchen und Gemeinden*, vol. 1: *Der Hauptgottesdienst mit Predigt und heiligem Abendmahl und die sonstigen Predigt- und Abendmahlsgottesdienste* (Berlin and Hamburg: Lutherisches Verlagshaus, 1955).

and, of course, the Latin of the Roman rite and other Western liturgical traditions.

There are stylistic features in all these liturgical languages that separate them from the ordinary languages of the people. This distance was often the result of linguistic developments in the common language that were not adopted in the liturgical language because of its stable nature. However, in the case of Latin as the language of the Roman liturgy, a certain distance existed right from the beginning: the Romans did not speak in the style of the Canon or of the Collects of the Mass. As soon as Greek was replaced by Latin in the Roman liturgy, a highly stylized medium of worship was created.

From Greek to Latin: The Language of the Roman Liturgy

The prevailing language of the first Christian communities in Rome was Greek. This is evident from Saint Paul's Letter to the Romans and from the earliest Christian literary works that originated in Rome, for instance, the *First Letter of Clement*, the *Shepherd of Hermas*, and the writings of Justin Martyr. In the first two centuries, there were several popes with Greek names, and Christian tomb inscriptions were written in Greek.[19] It would be reasonable to assume

[19] M. K. Lafferty, "Translating Faith from Greek to Latin: Romanitas and Christianitas in Late Fourth-Century Rome and Milan", *Journal of Early Christian Studies* 11 (2003): 29, notes that epitaphs continued to be in Greek even for popes with Latin names, Urbanus, Pontianus, Fabianus, and Lucius. The exception is Pope Cornelius (d. 253), whose epitaph is in Latin. On the presence of Greek-speaking Christians in Rome, see C. P. Caspari, *Ungedruckte, unbeachtete und wenig beachtete Quellen zur Geschichte des Taufsymbols und der Glaubensregel*, 3 vols. (Christiania: Malling, 1866–1875), 3:303–466, esp. 456–57.

that, during this period, Greek was also the common language of the Roman liturgy. The situation was probably similar in other parts of the Western Empire; for instance, Irenaeus, Bishop of Lyon, who died around the year 200, wrote in Greek. The shift toward Latin began, not in Rome, but in North Africa, where the "earliest known converts were Latin-speaking natives of the province rather than Greek-speaking immigrants."[20] From the middle of the second century, Latin translations of Greek texts emerged in Rome: Clement's *Letter to the Corinthians* and the vulgate version of the *Shepherd of Hermas*.[21] By the middle of the third century, this transition toward Latin in the Roman Church was well advanced: members of the Roman clergy wrote to Cyprian of Carthage in Latin; Latin was also the language in which Novatian composed his *De Trinitate* and other works, quoting from an existing Latin version of the Bible.[22] In addition, the stream of immigrants from the

---

[20] Lafferty, "Translating Faith", 29, n. 27, with reference to J. Rives, *Religion and Authority in Roman Carthage from Augustus to Constantine* (Oxford: Clarendon, 1995), 223–26. See also G. Bardy, *La question des langues dans l'Église ancienne*, Études de Théologie Historique (Paris: Beauchesne, 1948), 57–63.

[21] Bardy, *Question des langues*, 106–7.

[22] Note that the so-called *Traditio Apostolica*, attributed to Hippolytus of Rome, cannot be used as a source for Roman liturgical practice in this period because of uncertainties about its date, origin, and authorship. See B. Steimer, *Vertex traditionis: Die Gattung der altchristlichen Kirchenordnungen*, Beihefte zur Zeitschrift für die neutestamentliche Wissenschaft 63 (Berlin and New York: de Gruyter, 1992); M. Metzger, "À propos des règlements ecclésiastiques et de la prétendue *Tradition apostolique*", *Revue des sciences religieuses* 66 (1992): 249–61; C. Markschies, "Wer schrieb die sogenannte Traditio Apostolica? Neue Beobachtungen und Hypothesen zu einer kaum lösbaren Frage aus der altkirchlichen Literaturgeschichte", in *Tauffragen und Bekenntnis: Studien zur sogenannten "Traditio Apostolica", zu den "Interrogationes de fide" und zum "Römischen Glaubensbekenntnis"*, by C. Markschies, W. Kinzig, and M. Vinzent, Arbeiten zur Kirchengeschichte 74 (Berlin and New York:

East to Rome seems to have diminished in the second half of the third century. This demographic change meant that the life of the Roman Church began to be increasingly shaped by native Latin-speakers.

There is a passage from Marius Victorinus' *Adversus Arium*, book 2, written around 360, which is usually taken to indicate that Greek continued to be used in the Roman liturgy until the second half of the fourth century. Victorinus, writing in Rome in Latin, quotes from a Eucharistic Prayer (*oratio oblationis*): σῶσον περιούσιον λαόν, ζηλωτὴν καλῶν ἔργων—"save the people of thine own, zealous for good works", a phrase taken from Titus 2:14.[23] However, this evidence should not be taken at face value. The context for this quotation is Victorinus' defense of the Nicene ὁμοούσιος against those who argue that the word οὐσία/*substantia* is not found in Holy Scripture. He points to a similar use of language, that is, compound adjectives ending on –ούσιος: first, the petition from the Lord's Prayer, "Give us this day our daily bread" (ἐπιούσιος ἄρτος); then, Titus 2:14, where the redeemed are called λαὸς περιούσιος, "a people for his own possession"; and, finally, the *oratio oblationis* as quoted above.[24] In book 1 of *Adversus Arium*, Victorinus makes the same argument and adduces the same texts, but here his

de Gruyter, 1999), 1–79; and P. F. Bradshaw, M. E. Johnson, and L. E. Philips, *The Apostolic Tradition: A Commentary*, Hermeneia (Minneapolis, Minn.: Fortress Press, 2002). This most recent research confirms the insights of L. Bouyer, *Eucharist: Theology and Spirituality of the Eucharistic Prayer*, trans. C. U. Quinn (Notre Dame and London: University of Notre Dame Press, 1968), 188–91.

[23] Marius Victorinus, *Adversus Arium* II, 8: CSEL 83:182–83.

[24] This is a good example of the principle "ut legem credendi lex statuat supplicandi" later formulated by Prosper of Aquitaine (d. 455); see *Enchiridion symbolorum, defnitionum et declarationum de rebus fidei et morum*, ed. H. Denzinger and P. Hünermann, 40th rev. ed. (Freiburg: Herder, 2005), no. 246.

quotation from the Eucharistic Prayer is in Latin: "munda tibi populum circumvitalem, aemulatorem bonorum operum." Since the Latin word *circumvitalem* obviously does not help him to make his point, he adds the explanation "circa tuam substantiam venientem".[25] It does not seem clear whether the prayer cited by Marius Victorinus was actually said in Greek or in Latin, or perhaps in either language, in the various churches of Rome. The skilled rhetorician might have chosen to refer to a version of the prayer that had already fallen out of use by his time, in order to reinforce his argument in favor of the ὁμοούσιος. Moreover, it should be noted that the petition "save the people of thine own, zealous for good works" is echoed in the Prayers of the Faithful of the East Syrian rite,[26] but not in the later Roman rite.[27]

Equally difficult to interpret is the evidence from the works of the author known as Ambrosiaster, who was probably a Roman presbyter and wrote in the pontificate of Damasus (366–384).[28] The intriguing passages are found in Ambrosiaster's commentary on 1 Corinthians 14:[29]

---

[25] Marius Victorinus, *Adversus Arium* I, 30: CSEL 83:64.

[26] F. E. Brightman, *Liturgies Eastern and Western*, vol. 1 (Oxford: Clarendon Press, 1896), 264, l. 3.

[27] Hence the comment of Bardy, *Question des langues*, 163, is apposite: "Malgré tout, le témoignage de Victorinus est loin d'être décisif, et il est difficile d'en tirer quelque parti assuré."

[28] For a good overview of recent scholarship, see S. Lunn-Rockliffe, *Ambrosiaster's Political Theology*, Oxford Early Christian Studies (Oxford: Oxford University Press, 2007), 11–86.

[29] First Corinthians 14 has consistently been used as a reference in debates on liturgical language throughout Church history: in the dispute over the Old Slavonic liturgy introduced by Saints Cyril and Methodius, in the Protestant Reformation, and at the Council of Trent; see H. A. P. Schmidt, *Liturgie et langue vulgaire: Le problème de la langue liturgique chez les premiers Réformateurs et au Concile de Trente*, Analecta Gregoriana 53 (Rome: Apud Aedes Unversitatis Gregorianae, 1950).

> It is obvious that our mind (*animus*) is ignorant if it speaks in a tongue that it does not know, just as Latin-speakers are accustomed to chant in Greek, delighted by the sound of the words but nevertheless not knowing what they are saying. Therefore, the spirit (*spiritus*), which is bestowed in baptism, knows what the mind (*animus*) prays, while it speaks or prays in a language unknown to it; but the mind (*mens*), which is the *animus*, has no profit. For what profit can it gain if it does not know what it is saying?[30]

> ... They preferred to speak to the people in church in an unknown tongue, just as some Latin-speakers [prefer] the Creed (*symbolum*) in Greek.[31]

Here the Apostle Paul's reference to "speaking in tongues", *lingua* or *linguis loqui* in Ambrosiaster's (pre-Vulgate) Latin text, is taken to mean speaking in a foreign or unknown tongue. Hence the commentator can hardly be exonerated of the charge of twisting the biblical text, all the more since he seems to be aware that "speaking in tongues" is a particular charismatic phenomenon (*donum spiritus sancti*).[32] Ambrosiaster's comments would seem to reflect the situation in the pontificate of Damasus, when there were (still) communities in the largely Latin-speaking Roman Church

---

[30] Ambrosiaster, *In Epistulas ad Corinthios* I, 14, 14: CSEL 81/2:153: "Manifestum est ignorare animum nostrum, si lingua loquatur quam nescit, sicut adsolent Latini homines Graece cantare oblectati sono verborum, nescientes tamen quid dicant. spiritus ergo, qui datur in baptismo, scit quid oret animus, dum loquitur aut perorat lingua sibi ignota; mens autem, qui est animus, sine fructu est. quem enim potest habere profectum, qui ignorat quae loquatur?"; English translation from Lafferty, "Translating Faith from Greek to Latin", 32–33.

[31] Ambrosiaster, *In Epistulas ad Corinthios* I, 14, 19: CSEL 81/2:155: "Ignota sibi lingua loqui malebant in ecclesia ad populum quam sua, siut Latini symbolum Graece."

[32] Ibid., 14, 18: CSEL 81/2:154.

that prayed or, to be more precise, chanted in Greek. He notes disapprovingly that some are attached to this, because they enjoy its aesthetic appeal, while they do not understand the language. Ambrosiaster does not completely disapprove of this practice, since he concedes that one can still profit from it spiritually; however, he considers praying in a known language superior, because then the benefit is also on the intellectual or cognitive level. Ambrosiaster's motive for using the biblical text in such a polemical manner may be found farther below in his commentary (on verses 24–25):

> When [someone who is not a believer or who is not familiar with the Christian faith] understands, and understands by hearing, that God is being praised and that Christ is being adored, he sees clearly that this is the true and venerable religion, in which nothing is spurious, he sees that nothing is being done in secret, as among pagans, whose eyes are veiled, so that they do not perceive what they call "sacred" (*sacra*) and thus do not understand that they are ridiculed by various follies. For every impostor aims at obscurity and shows what is false as if it were true. Therefore among us nothing is done in a hidden way, nothing behind a veil; rather, praise is given in a simple manner to the one God, from whom all things are, and to the Lord Jesus, through whom all things are. For if there is no one he can understand or who refutes him, he can say that [our faith] is some sort of deception and folly, which would be shameful if were to be made public.[33]

Ambrosiaster was obviously anxious to set Christianity apart from contemporary mystery religions and thought that the use of a foreign language in worship would give the impression that the Christian faith was just another pagan

[33] Ibid., 14, 24–25: CSEL 81/2:157–58.

cult. In this context, the exegete was certainly an advocate for the use of Latin in the Roman liturgy of his time, because this made it more approachable.[34] The most interesting aspect of Ambrosiaster's comments is that they provide a rare glimpse into debates surrounding a historical transition that are otherwise not recorded.

In a work now also generally attributed to him,[35] the *Questions on the Old and the New Testaments*, Ambrosiaster gives another piece of interesting evidence: in a question where he proposes the eccentric interpretation of Melchisedek as a manifestation of the Holy Spirit, he refers to the Eucharistic Prayer in Rome, in which this enigmatic Old Testament figure is called *summus sacerdos*,[36] a title familiar from the established version of the Canon of the Mass.

The Roman Canon

The most important source for the Roman Eucharistic Prayer in the late fourth century is Saint Ambrose of Milan. In his *De sacramentis*, a series of catecheses for the newly baptized that was held around 390, Ambrose quotes extensively from the Eucharistic Prayer employed at that time in his city. The passages quoted are earlier forms of the prayers *Quam oblationem*, *Qui pridie*, *Unde et memores*, *Supra*

---

[34] Mohrmann's reading of Ambrosiaster is somewhat forced, but she is right to observe that his "argument is closely bound up with conditions prevailing at the time": *Liturgical Latin*, 52.

[35] Ambrosiaster was identified as the author of the *Quaestiones* by A. Souter, *A Study of Ambrosiaster*, Texts and Studies 7.4 (Cambridge: Cambridge University Press, 1905), whose arguments are now commonly accepted; cf. Lunn-Rockliffe, *Ambrosiaster's Political Theology*, 32.

[36] Ps.-Augustine, *Quaestiones veteris ac novi testamenti* 109, 21: CSEL 50:268.

quae, and *Supplices te rogamus*. Elsewhere in *De sacramentis*, the Bishop of Milan emphasizes that he desires to follow the use of the Roman Church in everything; for this reason, we can safely assume that the same Eucharistic Prayer he quotes was also used in Rome.[37] Since the first prayer Ambrose cites begins with the words "Fac nobis hanc oblationem ...", there must obviously have been a preceding prayer to which "this oblation" referred. Michael Moreton has presented a plausible hypothesis that is based on Ambrose's own comments in *De sacramentis* and on our knowledge of the later form of the Canon. He proposes that the earlier mention of the oblation

> ... can hardly have been anything else than the *Te igitur*, or something very like it, in view of Ambrose's earlier statement *oratio petitur pro populo, pro regibus, pro caeteris*. This *oratio* for those who constitute the communion of the Church is coupled in *Te igitur* with the Church's *dona, munera, sancta sacrificia illibata*, to which Ambrose refers as the *sacramenta posita super altare*. Further, Ambrose's reference to the angels who watched the approach of the neophytes from the baptistery to the altar, *spectarunt angeli*, may conceivably contain an allusion to the Pre-Sanctus at the conclusion of the *laus*, to which he refers in the clause *laus deo defertur*.[38]

There are also probable parallels to the Roman Canon in the sermons of Zeno, Bishop of Verona from 362 to 372: references to Melchisedek as *summus sacerdos* and to Abraham

[37] Ambrose, *De sacramentis* III, 1, 5: CSEL 73:40: "Ecclesia Romana ... cuius typum in omnibus sequimur et formam.... In omnibus cupio sequi ecclesiam Romanam." Explaining the baptismal ceremonies in Milan, Ambrose pays particular attention to the main point where he differs from Roman usage, that is, in the washing of the feet of the candidates.

[38] M.J. Moreton, "Rethinking the Origin of the Roman Canon", *Studia Patristica* 26 (1993): 65–66.

as *patriarcha noster*, like those in the *Supra quae* prayer, and a reference to *immaculata hostia*. This interesting evidence would testify to the geographical spread of this Eucharistic Prayer in an age when this very fact must be regarded as worthy of note.[39]

The wording of the prayers cited by Ambrose is different from the Canon that was settled by Pope Gregory the Great in the late sixth century and has come down to us, with only a few minor changes, in the oldest extant liturgical books, especially the Old Gelasian Sacramentary, dating from the middle of the eighth century, but believed to reflect the liturgical use of the middle of the seventh century (see chapter 3, appendix 1, below pp. 111–13). The differences between Ambrose's Eucharistic Prayer and the Gregorian Canon are far less remarkable than their similarities, since the almost three hundred years lying between the two texts were a period of intense liturgical development.[40] It is therefore most remarkable that a mature version of the Roman Canon emerges without any antecedents in the late fourth century.[41]

---

[39] G. Jeanes, "Early Latin Parallels to the Roman Canon? Possible References to a Eucharistic Prayer in Zeno of Verona", *Journal of Theological Studies*, n.s., 37 (1986): 427–31.

[40] Ambrose, *De sacramentis* IV, 5, 21–22; 6, 26–27: CSEL 73:55 and 57; see J. Beumer, "Die ältesten Zeugnisse für die römische Eucharistiefeier bei Ambrosius von Mailand", *Zeitschrift für katholische Theologie* 95 (1973): 311–24; Bouley, *From Freedom to Formula*, 200–215. The term "canon" seems to have been used first in the sixth century; the oldest known reference to "prex canonica" is Pope Vigilius, *Ep. ad Profuturum* 5: PL 69:18; see Bouley, *From Freedom to Formula*, 208–9.

[41] Cf. Botte–Mohrmann, *Ordinaire de la messe*, 17: "C'est à la fin du quatrième siècle que le Canon Romain sort des ténèbres de sa préhistoire." There are passages in Tertullian that are reminiscent of the prayer language of the Roman Canon; these were identified by E. Dekkers, *Tertullianus en de geschiedenis der liturgie*, Catholica 6, 2 (Brussels: De Kinkhoren; Amsterdam: Desclée de Brouwer, 1947), 56–58. These passages may have been quotations from or

Anton Baumstark argued for an older Greek version of the Canon, taking his clue from *summus sacerdos*, which he considered an erroneous translation of the Greek text that would have followed the Septuagint reading of Genesis 14:18, ἦν δὲ ἱερεὺς τοῦ θεοῦ τοῦ ὑψίστου, "he was priest of God the Most High".[42] The eminent liturgist conjectured that the original would have read something like τὴν προσφορὰν Μελχισεδὲκ τοῦ ἱερέως σοῦ τοῦ ὑψίστου. The Latin translator would have misconstrued the reference to Melchisedek as "the most high priest of God", hence the translation "quod tibi obtulit summus sacerdos tuus Melchisedech".[43] Bernard Botte objected that a passage in the late-fourth-century *Apostolic Constitutions* also referred to Melchisedek as "high priest" (τὸν Μελχισεδὲκ ἀρχιερέα). This would indicate that this attribution had already obtained some currency in the Christian East by the time the phrase *summus sacerdos* emerged in Latin and was not necessarily an indication of a translation error.[44] However, Baumstark replied

allusions to contemporary Eucharistic Prayers, which were then (as prayer texts) incorporated into the Roman Canon. An alternative explanation would be that whoever composed the Canon deliberately took these phrases from Tertullian, without there being continuity between earlier North African Anaphoras and the later *Canon Missae*. Cf. M. Klöckener, "Das eucharistische Hochgebet in der nordafrikanischen Liturgie der christlichen Spätantike", in *Prex eucharistica*, vol. 3: *Studia*, pt. 1: *Ecclesia antiqua et occidentalis*, ed. A. Gerhards, H. Brakmann, and M. Klöckener, Spicilegium Friburgense 42 (Fribourg: Academic Press, 2005), 53 (with n. 59), who opts for the second explanation.

[42] See, for instance, Tertullian, *Adversus Iudaeos* 2, 14: CCSL 2:1344: "Melchisedek quoque, summi Dei sacerdos".

[43] A. Baumstark, "Ein Übersetzungsfehler im Meßkanon", *Studia catholica* 5 (1928): 378–82, and *Missale Romanum: Seine Entwicklung, ihre wichtigsten Urkunden und Probleme* (Eindhoven and Nijmegen: van Eupen, 1929), 13.

[44] *Apostolic Constitutions* VIII, 12, 23: SC 336:188; cf. B. Botte, *Le Canon de la messe romaine*, Textes et études liturgiques 2 (Louvain: Abbaye du Mont César, 1935), 42.

by proposing that the Latin Canon had already been formed by the middle of the third century and was thus considerably earlier than the *Apostolic Constitutions*.[45] In fact, he contended that the Latin text of this Eucharistic Prayer may have been introduced in Rome not long after the pontificate of Cornelius (251–253), the first pope whose epitaph was composed in Latin.[46] While it would seem very unlikely that the Roman Eucharistic Prayer would have been used in Latin as early as the middle of the third century,[47] parts of it certainly include some very ancient material.

Most interestingly, the post-Institution Narrative prayers *Unde et memores* and *Supra quae* contain elements that are taken from an early Judaeo-Christian background: in the first prayer it is above all the idea of a pure, holy, and perfect sacrifice (*hostiam puram, hostiam sanctam, hostiam immaculatam*), which corresponds to ancient Jewish interpretations of the sacrifice of Isaac, beginning with Philo of Alexandria.[48] In the *Supra quae* prayer, there is the striking notion

---

[45] A. Baumstark, "Antik-römischer Gebetsstil im Messkanon", in *Miscellanea Liturgica in honorem L. C. Mohlberg*, vol. 1, Bibliotheca Ephemerides liturgicae 22 (Rome: Ed. Liturgiche, 1948), 301–5.

[46] A. Baumstark, "Das 'Problem' des römischen Messkanons, eine Retractatio auf geistesgeschichtlichem Hintergrund", *Ephemerides liturgicae* 53 (1939): 242–43. Cornelius is named last in the list of popes invoked in the *Communicantes* section of the Canon; he is placed after Sixtus, who suffered martyrdom in 258. This was done presumably in order to associate him with his contemporary and correspondent Cyprian of Carthage (d. 258). Cf. N.J. Roy, "The Roman Canon: *deësis* in euchological form", in *Benedict XVI and the Sacred Liturgy*, ed. N.J. Roy and J.E. Rutherford (Dublin: Four Courts Press, 2010), 191.

[47] Cf. C. Mohrmann, "Quelques observations sur l'évolution stylistique du Canon de la Messe romain", in *Études sur le latin des chrétiens*, 3:230–31.

[48] Cf. F. Manns, "L'origine judéo-chrétienne de la prière 'Unde et memores' du Canon Romain", *Ephemerides Liturgicae* 101 (1987): 60–68, esp. 64–67.

of the "altar on high" (cf. Rev 8:3)[49] to which the "holy angel"—Christ himself, the "angelus magni consilii" (Is 9:6), according to primitive Angel-Christology[50]—is asked to carry the Church's oblation. The references to Abel, Abraham, and Melchisedek are deeply rooted in Jewish tradition, particularly in Temple worship,[51] and the fact that these pre-Mosaic sacrifices are construed as types of the Eucharist would seem to indicate an apologetic context, such as the second century, when Christian authors insisted that the Levitical sacrifices were no longer acceptable to God and saw in the sacrifices of Abel, Abraham, and especially Melchisedek, offering bread and wine, fitting types of the Eucharist.[52]

Liturgical scholars have tended to emphasize the disparate nature of the Roman Canon and have used the methods of higher criticism to explain the origin and development of its prayers. With a view to such hypothetical reconstructions (including his own), Anton Baumstark published a

[49] Irenaeus of Lyon, *Adversus Haereses* IV, 18, 6: SC 100:614, writes: "Est ergo altare in caelis, illuc enim preces nostrae et oblationes diriguntur; et templum, quemadmodum Iohannes in Apocalypsi ait." This idea is already implicit in Clement of Rome, who calls Jesus Christ "the high priest of our offerings"; *1 Clement* 36:1–2: SC 167:158.

[50] Cf. Justin Martyr, *Dialogue with Trypho* 76, 3, and 126, 1: ed. M. Marcovich, Patristische Texte und Studien 47, 201 and 288; also *1 Apology* 63, 5: ed. M. Marcovich, Patristische Texte und Studien 38, 121; Irenaeus of Lyon, *Adversus Haereses* III, 16, 3: SC 34:283 and *Demonstratio* 55–56: SC 406:162. It is significant that this passage is modified in Ambrose's Eucharistic Prayer to the plural "per manus angelorum tuorum" (*De sacramentis* IV, 6, 27: CSEL 73:57), presumably because by the late fourth century, Angel-Christology had acquired an "Arian" flavor.

[51] B. Bagatti, "L'origine gerosolimitana della preghiera Supra quae del Canone Romano", *Bibbia e Oriente* 21 (1979): 101–8, and F. Manns, "Une prière judéo-chrétienne dans le Canon Romain", *Antonianum* 54 (1979): 3–9.

[52] Cf. G. G. Willis, *A History of Early Roman Liturgy to the Death of Pope Gregory the Great*, Henry Bradshaw Society, Subsidia 1 (London: Boydell Press, 1994), 30–31.

remarkable retraction, in which he proposes to consider the Canon in its integrity[53] and explores its parallels in contents, structure, and expression with the Eucharistic Prayer of the Egyptian or, more precisely, the Alexandrian tradition.[54] The Roman Canon was obviously not created *ex nihilo*, and its parallels with Greek anaphoral prayers would seem to point to more ancient common sources.[55]

A Christian Latin Culture

Returning to the question of language, according to Optatus of Milevis, writing in the 360s, there were more than forty churches in Rome already before the Constantinian settlement.[56] Hence it would be reasonable to assume that there were Latin-speaking communities in the third century, if not before. Parts of the liturgy were already in Latin before the second half of the fourth century, notably the readings from Holy Scripture. By the late fourth century,

---

[53] See Baumstark, "'Problem' des römischen Messkanons", passim. For various earlier hypotheses of reconstructing the "original" Roman Canon, see the good overview of A. Fortescue, *The Mass: A Study of the Roman Liturgy*, 2nd ed. (London: Longmans, Green and Co, 1950), 138–71. On this subject, see also G. G. Willis, "The Connection of the Prayers of the Roman Canon", *Essays in Early Roman Liturgy*, Alcuin Club Collections 46 (London: SPCK, 1964), 121–33.

[54] Cf. Bouyer, *Eucharist*, 187–243, who undertakes a similar comparison and concludes that "the Roman canon appears ... as one of the most venerable witnesses of the oldest tradition of the eucharistic prayer, at least contemporary in its totality with the most archaic forms of the Alexandrian eucharist" (243).

[55] Moreton, "Rethinking the Origin of the Roman Canon", 66, concludes that "the Latin canon in its earliest form, in Milan and therefore in Rome, was not a creation *de novo*, but was indebted to older anaphoral prayers, not only in the East, and perhaps especially in Egypt, but also in the Greek-speaking Church in the West."

[56] Optatus, *Contra Parmenidem* II, 4: CSEL 26:39.

the ancient version of the psalms used in the liturgy had acquired such a sacrosanct status that Saint Jerome revised it only with caution. Later he translated the Psalter from the Hebrew, as he said, not for liturgical purposes, but to provide a text for scholarship and controversy.[57]

Mohrmann introduces a useful distinction between: first, "purely prayer texts", where language is, above all, a medium of expression; secondly, texts that are "destined to be read, the Epistle and Gospel"; and, thirdly, "confessional texts", such as the Creed. In "prayer texts we are concerned with expressional form; in the others, primarily with forms of communication".[58] Recent research on language and ritual, such as the work of Catherine Bell, confirms Mohrmann's insight that language has different functions in different parts of the liturgy, which go beyond mere communication or information.[59] These theoretical reflections help us to understand the development of the early Roman liturgy: those parts where the element of communication was prevalent, such as the Scripture readings, were translated earlier, whereas the Eucharistic Prayer continued to be said in Greek for a much longer period.

To conclude this discussion, the available evidence strongly suggests that the transition from Greek to Latin in the Roman liturgy happened slowly and gradually.[60] This development

[57] See Jerome's two prefaces to the Psalter in *Biblia sacra iuxta Vulgatam versionem*, ed. R. Weber and R. Gryson, 4th ed. (Stuttgart: Deutsche Bibelgesellschaft, 1994), 767–69; cf. C. Mohrmann, "The New Latin Psalter: Its Diction and Style", in *Études sur le latin des chrétiens*, 2:110–11.

[58] Mohrmann, *Liturgical Latin*, 75, detects this distinction already in Christian antiquity.

[59] C. Bell, *Ritual: Perspectives and Dimensions* (New York: Oxford University Press, 1997).

[60] Mohrmann, *Liturgical Latin*, 50–53; J. A. Jungmann, *Missarum Sollemnia: Eine genetische Erklärung der römischen Messe*, 2 vols., 5th ed. (Vienna: Herder,

took more than a hundred years and was completed in the pontificate of Damasus, who died in 384. From then on, the liturgy in Rome was celebrated mostly in Latin, with the exception of a few remainders of the older use, such as the Greek readings in the Papal Mass.[61] As for the intriguing question of why the move toward a Latin liturgy in Rome occurred rather late, various answers have been given, and there is something to be said for all of them. The German liturgist Theodor Klauser attributed this to the general

---

1962), 1:65–66; Bouley, *From Freedom to Formula*, 203–7; *pace* T. Klauser, "Der Übergang der römischen Kirche von der griechischen zur lateinischen Liturgiesprache", in *Miscellanea Giovanni Mercati: 1. Bibbia, letteratura cristiana antica*, Studi e testi 121 (Vatican City: Biblioteca Apostolica Vaticana, 1946), 467–82. Against Klauser's hypothesis that the Latin Canon of the Mass came from Milan, see C. Mohrmann, "*Rationabilis*—λογικός", in *Études sur le latin des chrétiens*, 1:179–87.

[61] In later periods, Greek elements were introduced into the Roman liturgy again, most notably the invocation *Kyrie eleison* as part of the Latin litany known as *Deprecatio Gelasii* and named after Pope Gelasius (492–496); cf. Bardy, *Question des langues*, 164, n. 2, and B. Capelle, "Le Kyrie de la messe et le pape Gélase", *Révue Bénédictine* 46 (1934): 126–44. In the seventh century, there was a strong influx of Eastern Christians in Rome, which is reflected in the adoption of the *Trisagion* in the *Improperia* of the Good Friday liturgy and the use of bilingual readings on several solemn celebrations in the liturgical year, such as Christmas and Easter (Sunday and Monday), the Vigils of Easter and Pentecost, the four Ember Saturdays, and the Mass for the ordination of a pope; cf. C. Vogel, *Medieval Liturgy: An Introduction to the Sources*, rev. and trans. W. G. Storey and N. K. Rasmussen (Washington, D.C.: Pastoral Press, 1986), 296–97. An intriguing case is the so-called *Missa graeca*, which is attested in several manuscripts from the Carolingian age. Texts of the Roman Ordinary of the Mass are written in Greek but in Latin letters, and they are sometimes provided with neumes, indicating that they would have been sung. See C. M. Atkinson, "Missa graeca", in *Messe und Motette*, ed. L. Lütteken, MGG prisma (Kassel: Bärenreiter; Stuttgart: Metzler, 2002), 18–19. This phenomenon spread throughout Europe even to places where Greek culture was quite remote and illustrates the prestige of Greek as a liturgical language in Western Christendom; cf. W. Berschin, *Griechisch-lateinisches Mittelalter: Von Hieronymus zu Nikolaus von Kues* (Bern and Munich: Francke, 1980), 31–38.

conservatism of Romans and their tenacity in keeping religious traditions. This is certainly true for the Roman Church as well. On the other hand, according to the American Benedictine Allan Bouley, the need for a carefully formulated orthodox language, especially during the Arian crisis of the fourth century, provided the leaven for creating an official Latin form of the prayers of the Mass. Bouley's thesis is certainly borne out by Ambrose's efforts to formulate the Trinitarian faith in liturgical hymns against the current Arianism of the barbarian tribes. Further, Christine Mohrmann argues that the formation of liturgical Latin became possible only after the Peace of the Church, established by Emperor Constantine. There was no longer such a strong need for Christian communities to define themselves in opposition to the surrounding pagan culture. Their new secure status gave the local churches in the West greater freedom to draw, at least for purposes of style, if not of content, on the religious heritage of Rome for the development of their liturgies.

Finally, Peter Burke, a major contributor to the relatively new academic discipline of "sociolinguistics", or the "social history of language", has alerted us to the fact that "the choice of one language over another is never a neutral or transparent one."[62] Hence, it is important to consider the transition from Greek to Latin in the Roman liturgy in its historical, social, and cultural context. The formation of a Latin liturgical language should be seen as part of a wide-ranging effort to Christianize Roman culture. The pontificate of Damasus, who commissioned Jerome to produce a new

[62] In the words of Lafferty, "Translating Faith from Greek to Latin", 24, referring to P. Burke, *The Art of Conversation* (Ithaca: Cornell University Press, 1993).

Latin version of the Holy Scriptures, which came to be known as the "Vulgate", was a milestone on the way toward a Christian *Latinitas*. It is significant that the shift toward a Latin liturgy in Rome was completed during the reign of this pope of Spanish background. The importance of Damasus' own contribution to this is disputed by scholars; Klauser credits him with the initiative to determine Latin as the "new" liturgical language, whereas Bernard Botte and Charles Pietri argue more convincingly that Damasus' pontificate saw the conclusion of a development that had been underway for a considerable time.[63] In the second half of the fourth century, the leading bishops in Italy, above all Damasus in Rome and Ambrose in Milan, were striving to Christianize the culture of their day. In the city of Rome, there was a strong pagan presence, and especially the aristocracy continued to adhere to pagan customs, even if they had become nominal Christians.[64] Rome was no longer the center of political power, but its culture continued to have a hold on the thought-world of its elite; in fact the fourth century is now considered a period of literary renaissance, with a renewed interest in the "classics" of Roman poetry and prose. There was even a

---

[63] A decisive role in the introduction of the Latin liturgy is attributed to Pope Damasus by Klauser, "Der Übergang der römischen Kirche", and M. H. Shepherd, "The Liturgical Reform of Damasus I", in *Kyriakon: Festschrift Johannes Quasten*, ed. P. Granfield and J. A. Jungmann, 2 vols. (Münster: Aschendorff, 1970), 2:847–63. For a different analysis with less emphasis on Damasus' contribution, see Botte–Mohrmann, *Ordinaire de la messe*, 17, and C. Pietri, "Damase évêque de Rome", in *Saecularia Damasiana: Atti del convegno internazionale per il XVI centenario della morte di Papa Damaso I (11–12–384—10/12–12–1984)*, Studi di antichità cristiana 39 (Vatican City: Pontificio Istituto di Archeologia Cristiana, 1986), 50.

[64] On the difficulty of defining Christian identity in the late Roman Empire, see R. Marcus, *The End of Ancient Christianity* (Cambridge: Cambridge University Press, 1990), 19–83.

revival of Latin in the eastern half of the empire. The emperors of the fourth century certainly cultivated this *Latinitas*.[65] With characteristic tenacity, Rome kept its ancient traditions.

The popes of the late fourth century and of the fifth century, beginning with Damasus, made a conscious and comprehensive attempt to appropriate the symbols of Roman culture for the Christian faith. Part of this attempt was the appropriation of public space through extensive building projects. After the Constantinian dynasty had taken the lead with the monumental basilicas of the Lateran and Saint Peter's, as well as the cemetery basilicas outside the city walls, later emperors and popes continued this building program that was to make Rome into a city dominated by churches. Perhaps the most prestigious project was the construction of a new basilica dedicated to Saint Paul's on the Via Ostiensis, replacing the small Constantinian edifice by a new church that would match the size of Saint Peter's.[66] Another important aspect was the appropriation of public time with a cycle of Christian feasts throughout the year replacing pagan celebrations, as with the Philocalian calendar of the year 354. The formation of liturgical Latin was part of this effort to evangelize Roman culture and attract the influential elites of the empire to the Christian faith. It would

---

[65] See Lafferty, "Translating Faith from Greek to Latin", 26–28, with references to A. Cameron, "Latin Revival of the Fourth Century", in *Renaissances before the Renaissance: Cultural Revivals of Late Antiquity and the Middle Ages*, ed. W. Treadgold (Stanford: Stanford University Press, 1984), 42–58, and C. W. Hedrick, *History and Silence: Purge and Rehabilitation of Memory in Late Antiquity* (Austin: University of Texas Press, 2000). On the presence of the Latin language in the eastern half of the Roman Empire in the fourth century, see also Bardy, *Question des langues*, 123–25 and 146–47.

[66] See the now beautifully illustrated volume of H. Brandenburg, *Die frühchristlichen Kirchen in Rom*, 2nd ed. (Regensburg: Schnell und Steiner, 2005).

not be accurate to describe this process simply as the adoption of the "vernacular" language in the liturgy, if by vernacular is meant colloquial. The Latin of the Canon, of the Collects, and the Prefaces of the Mass was removed from the idiom of the ordinary people. It was a highly stylized language that would have been difficult to understand by the average Roman Christian of the fifth century or later, especially since the rate of literacy was very low compared to our times.[67] And we should also remember that the adoption of *Latinitas* in the West made the liturgy more accessible to most people in Milan or Rome, but not necessarily to those whose native language was Gothic, Celtic, Iberic, or Punic.

It was by no means a foregone conclusion that the Western church would adopt Latin as its liturgical language. It is possible to imagine it using local languages in its liturgy, as in the East, where, in addition to Greek, Syriac, Coptic, Armenian, Georgian, and Ethiopic was used. However, the situation in the West was fundamentally different; the centralizing force of the Roman Church was such that Latin became the only liturgical language. This was an important factor in furthering ecclesiastical, cultural, and political unity. *Latinitas* became one of the defining characteristics of Western Europe.[68]

---

[67] Mohrmann, *Liturgical Latin*, 53–54; see also M. Klöckener, "Zeitgemäßes Beten: Meßorationen als Zeugnisse einer sich wandelnden Kultur und Spiritualität", in *Bewahren und Erneuern: Studien zur Meßliturgie: Festschrift für Hans Bernhard Meyer SJ zum 70. Geburtstag*, ed. R. Meßner, E. Nagel, and R. Pacik, Innsbrucker theologische Studien 42 (Innsbruck and Vienna: Tyrolia, 1995), 126–27.

[68] As Mohrmann, "The Ever-Recurring Problem of Language", 152, notes, "Liturgical Latin was not brought to these people as an isolated linguistic phenomenon. At the same time, Latin was introduced as the language of higher civilisation, of the schools, and of ecclesiastical and governmental administration. Thus all through the Middle Ages, Latin as the language of the sacred liturgy was supported by Latin as the second language of the cultural élite."

III

RHETORIC OF SALVATION

In this chapter, I shall discuss essential characteristics of the Latin idiom that became a distinct feature of the Roman liturgy in late antiquity. My analysis will focus on the question of how certain elements of style and rhetoric in liturgical prayers are employed to express theological ideas. The examples that will be presented here are taken from the Canon of the Mass and from a few chosen prayers from early sacramentaries. The great number of rhetorical devices in these texts marks them as belonging to the world of antiquity, where any literary text was formed according to technical rules of composition.[1] This was no different with Christian authors who were trained in the secular schools of rhetoric that were flourishing in the Roman Empire and were considered the climax of education. Many Church Fathers who had received a classical education, such as Gregory of Nazianzus and John Chrysostom in the East or Ambrose of Milan and Leo the Great in the West, made

[1] Cf. E. Norden, *Die antike Kunstprosa vom VI. Jahrhundert v. Chr. bis in die Zeit der Renaissance*, 2 vols., 2nd ed. (Leipzig: Teubner, 1909), 2:457, and C. Mohrmann, "Problèmes stylistiques dans la littérature latine chrétienne", in *Études sur le latin des chrétiens*, 4 vols., Storia e letteratura 65, 87, 103, 143 (Rome: Edizioni di Storia e Letteratura, 1961–1977), 3:147–48.

use of rhetorical devices quite naturally in their sermons and writings. Notably, in the fourth book of his *De doctrina christiana*, written in 426/427,[2] Augustine provided a theoretical foundation as to how a Christian "teacher" could employ the tools of rhetoric in order to communicate the truth in the most effective way possible.

Liturgical prayer is a form of public speech, and hence it is not surprising that in Christian antiquity, the threefold *officia* of classical rhetoric were applied to it as well. The reasons for this are presented succinctly by Mary Gonzaga Haessly in her seminal, though virtually unobtainable, work on *Rhetoric in the Sunday Collects of the Roman Missal*:

> All these devices of the art of language are necessary for us, for they enable us: (1) to grasp clearly the lessons embodied in the Prayers (docere); (2) to make these lessons more acceptable to us through the charm of diction and structure, in a word, through their appeal to our aesthetic sense (delectare); (3) to persuade us (movere) to mold our conduct in accordance with the principles of faith set forth in the Prayers. This explains why rhetoric is, and must be, found in the liturgy: it is to dispose us to pray "ut oportet," as we ought to pray.[3]

A rhetorical analysis also needs to consider the relationship between author (or speaker) and audience, but in the case of the liturgy, this raises a number of problems.[4] In the first place, the authorship of liturgical prayers is usually not

---

[2] Augustine, *De doctrina christiana* IV, 4–5 (ii, 3): ed. and trans. R. P. H. Green (Oxford: Clarendon Press, 1995), 196–98.

[3] M. G. Haessly, *Rhetoric in the Sunday Collects of the Roman Missal: With Introduction, Text, Commentary and Translation* (Cleveland: Ursuline College for Women, 1938), 5.

[4] Cf. P. Mack, "Rhetoric and Liturgy", in *Language and the Worship of the Church*, ed. D. Jasper and R. C. D. Jasper, Studies in Literature and Religion (Basingstoke: Macmillan, 1990), 86.

known. There is an interesting comment in Gregory the Great's letter to John, Bishop of Syracuse, dating from October 598, in which the Pope explains the reasons why he moved the Lord's Prayer in the Roman rite from its previous position before the Kiss of Peace and Holy Communion so that it would now follow immediately after the Canon, where it still is today.[5] Gregory considered it very unfitting that the "*prex*", which was composed by some "*scholasticus*", should be said over the oblation, while the prayer composed by our Redeemer should not be said over his own Body and Blood.[6] The term *scholasticus* in late ancient Latin could indicate an advocate or, more generally, a scholar or learned man. In the context of Gregory's letter, it may well refer to an official of the papal chancery who was in charge of composing or revising liturgical prayers or, indeed, of putting together the Mass *libelli* that were the sources for the major sacramentaries. In many cases, a *scholasticus* may simply have written down the prayers composed by popes such as Leo, Gelasius, and Gregory himself. Various historians of the liturgy have attempted to identify particular authors of prayers or even whole Mass formularies (see more on this below).

Likewise, the question of the "audience" is a complex one; no doubt, liturgical prayers were originally composed for a specific assembly, in whose presence and name they were addressed to God. However, the use of these prayers soon transcended limits of space and time. In fact, the oldest euchological texts of the Roman rite are of such a general

[5] G. G. Willis, "St Gregory the Great and the Lord's Prayer in the Roman Mass", in *Further Essays in Early Roman Liturgy*, Alcuin Club Collections 50 (London: SPCK, 1968), 175–88.

[6] Gregory the Great, *Ep.* IX, 26, Monumenta Germaniae Historica, Gregorii I Papae Registrum Epistolarum, 2:59–60.

nature that they could easily speak on behalf of different people in different situations and have done so ever since. These universal features of the Roman rite, along with its "simplicity" (in comparison to the more elaborate Eastern rites), made its wide diffusion possible. There are other elements, however, that show the rite's origin in the Church of Rome, such as the lists of saints in the Canon of the Mass or the Collect for the Solemnity of Saints Peter and Paul,[7] and thus express the local churches' communion with the Apostolic See.

For the purpose of this study, the question of authorship and audience are secondary; whoever may actually for the first time have formulated or recorded these texts for whatever particular congregation, once they entered the official liturgical books, they became part of Church's living tradition and were handed down, sometimes with modifications, as her solemn voice of prayer. The analysis presented in this chapter does not aim at completeness but, rather, wants to illustrate by way of chosen examples how this "rhetoric of salvation" works to achieve its threefold end of teaching the faith, giving spiritual delight, and persuading to a virtuous life.

The Canon of the Mass

In the following analysis, the Canon of the Mass will be taken as a unity; with this methodological approach, the

[7] This prayer, which is found in early Roman sacramentaries, contains the petition: "Da Ecclesiae tuae eorum in omnibus sequi praeceptum, per quos religionis sumpsit exordium" (Grant that your Church may in all things follow the teaching of those through whom she received the beginnings of her religion); cf. *Missale Romanum* 1570/1962, *Missale Romanum* 1970/2008, and *Roman Missal* 2011.

text of the ancient Eucharistic Prayer will be considered in its definitive form, which was established by Pope Gregory the Great and has been handed down from him with few minor modifications. Thus I shall not engage in discussions of the possible origin of the Canon's various prayers and their hypothetical dislocations (this subject has been touched upon in the previous chapter). Moreover, this is not a comparative study, and for this reason reference will be made to other Anaphoras, whether Eastern or Western, only when they contribute to a better understanding of the Roman Canon's linguistic characteristics.

Since we are in the fortunate position of having a primitive version of the Canon that is attested in Ambrose's *De sacramentis*, it will be useful to compare these two texts, because they are testimonies to a linguistic development that helps to highlight the characteristic features of the Roman euchological style (see appendix 1, below, pp. 111–13).[8]

Quam Oblationem

Ambrose's citation begins with the prayer "Fac nobis hanc oblationem ..." (Make this oblation ...). The use of the demonstrative pronoun indicates that there must have been preceding parts to which "this oblation" refers. As already

[8] This analysis is based on C. Mohrmann, *Liturgical Latin: Its Origins and Character: Three Lectures* (London: Burns & Oates, 1959); B. Botte and C. Mohrmann, *L'ordinaire de la messe: Texte critique, traduction et études*, Études liturgiques 2 (Paris: Cerf; Louvain: Abbaye du Mont César, 1953); and G. G. Willis, *A History of Early Roman Liturgy to the Death of Pope Gregory the Great*, Henry Bradshaw Society, Subsidia 1 (London: Boydell Press, 1994); cf. also the observations of A. Baumstark, "Antik-römischer Gebetsstil im Messkanon", in *Miscellanea Liturgica in honorem L. C. Mohlberg*, vol. 1, Bibliotheca Ephemerides liturgicae 22 (Rome: Ed. Liturgiche, 1948), 301–31.

mentioned in the previous chapter, it is quite probable that this was something very like the *Te igitur* of the later Gregorian Canon.

One notable revision is the replacement of paratactic constructions by a relative clause that links the sections of the Eucharistic Prayer. Thus the Ambrosian "Fac nobis hanc oblationem scriptam, rationabilem, acceptabilem" was changed to "Quam oblationem tu, Deus, in omnibus, quaesumus, benedictam, adscriptam, ratam, rationabilem acceptabilemque facere digneris" (Be pleased, O God, we pray, to bless, acknowledge, and approve this offering in every respect; make it spiritual and acceptable).[9] Through this revision, a strong grammatical link is established between two sections of the Canon.

The addition of "tu, Deus" and "in omnibus" is an embellishment on stylistic grounds that makes the form of the prayer appear more rounded and graceful. The verb *dignare* is taken from curial style and often found in papal correspondence.[10]

In this section of the Canon, we can observe another characteristic of Roman euchological style: series of consecutive synonyms or near-synonyms. A striking example

---

[9] The translations of the Roman Canon are taken from *Roman Missal* 2011, with occasional slight modifications to highlight particular features of the Latin original.

[10] *Dignare* is etymologically related to "deign", a word that was considered but ultimately rejected in the new official English-language version of the Roman Canon. For an insight into the difficulties of translation, see A. Roche, "Search for Truth and Poetry", *The Tablet*, August 5, 2006, 11: "Early in the process, we proposed that the priest should say: 'To us sinners also . . . deign to grant some share and fellowship with your holy apostles and martyrs.' 'Deign' was greeted with howls of derision from all sides: it was thought to belong to too formal a register for the liturgy. So we tried a much more colloquial version, 'please grant some share and fellowship'. This was judged too informal. So we finally settled on 'be pleased to grant', which seems to fall between the two."

of the use of adjectives with a similar meaning is found in the earliest Ambrosian version, where there are three epithets governing the substantive *oblationem*: *scriptam*, *rationabilem*, *acceptabilem*. In the later form of the prayer *Quam oblationem*, their number is increased to five: *benedictam*, *adscriptam*, *ratam*, *rationabilem*, *acceptabilemque*. This accumulation of adjectives that are virtually synonymous helps to make the language of the prayer more solemn and rhetorically effective. Note also the use of legal terms, such as *ratam* (approved).[11] For further patterns of juridical style, Mohrmann points to the conjunctions *nec non et* and *sed et*. However, these are found in classical authors like Cicero, Virgil, Suetonius, and Juvenal, and it would seem that they are simply a feature of later Latin rather than a borrowing from Roman legal language.

The prayer cited by Ambrose qualifies the offering as "figura corporis et sanguinis Domini nostri Iesu Christi". The formula "*figura*/ὁμοίωμα/ἀντίτυπον" of the Body/Blood of Christ is found in both Western and Eastern sources as early as Tertullian and the so-called *Apostolic Tradition*. Victor Saxer has argued that it forms part of the common core of early Eucharistic Prayers and may go back to the middle of the second century.[12] The use of *figura* should not be construed as denying the reality of the eucharistic presence of Christ's Body and Blood. It is rather a key term of typological exegesis, which sees in the Old Testament anticipa-

[11] Mohrmann, *Liturgical Latin*, 60, observes: "This monumental verbosity coupled with juridical precision . . . was the typical form of expression of the old Roman prayer."

[12] V. Saxer, "'Figura Corporis et Sanguinis Domini': Une formule eucharistique des premiers siècles chez Tertullian, Hippolyte et Ambroise", *Rivista di archeologia cristiana* 48 (1971): 65–89 (= *Pères saints et culte chrétien dans l'Église des premiers siècles*, Collected Studies Series 448 [Aldershot: Variorum, 1994], no. IV).

anticipations or prefigurations of the New and in the New Testament itself prefigurations of eschatological realities.

Ambrose cites the formula as traditional but does not use it to explain the presence of Christ in the sacrament; instead, when he comments on the eucharistic Consecration, he insists that the elements of bread and wine have been changed (*transfigurare*, *mutare*) into the Lord's Body and Blood.[13] Ambrose's theology appears to have had an impact on the revision of the Roman Canon, which includes an implicit epiclesis asking that the offering "may become for us the Body and Blood of your most beloved Son, our Lord Jesus Christ".

Institution Narrative

Both in Ambrose's Eucharistic Prayer and in the Gregorian Canon, the Institution Narrative begins with the relative pronoun *qui* that connects the whole section grammatically with the preceding prayer.

In most historical Anaphoras, the Institution Narrative rests on a liturgical tradition that is independent of the Synoptic Gospels (Mt 26:26–28; Mk 14:22–24; Lk 22:19–21). In many Eastern Eucharistic Prayers, the Narrative is greatly embellished and rhetorically stylized, such as in the Anaphoras of Saint Mark, Saint Basil, and especially Saint James. There are traits of such formalization in the Narrative of *De sacramentis*, where the introduction to the dominical words over the bread and over the chalice is constructed in parallel fashion ("pridie quam pateretur . . . respexit ad caelum,

[13] This is shown, with many references from Ambrose, by Saxer, "'Figura Corporis'", 79–84.

ad te, sancte Pater omnipotens aeterne Deus . . ."). By comparison with the some oriental Anaphoras, the Narrative in Ambrose is simple and sober in character, but it nonetheless shows signs of careful composition.

This is quite different in the Roman Canon, which, as E. C. Ratcliff notes, "presents the Gospel tradition on a bolder relief than we have it in the oriental forms or in *De Sacramentis*".[14] Ratcliff argues that the Roman Narrative is not a combination of the narratives found in the Synoptics; rather, it follows in essence that of Matthew 26:26–28, though not in the familiar Vulgate version, but in that of the Old Latin Gospels. Furthermore, the Narrative is supplemented with distinctive elements of 1 Corinthians 11:23–26 in the words over the cup and in the Lord's command to repeat this (action) in memory of him. There are also a few additions to the biblical account, which serve to "enhance the vividness of the Narrative and to educe ... the full significance of the Institution".[15] Most of them are, in fact, derived from Scripture, such as "elevatis oculis in caelum" (Mt 14:19, Mk 7:34; Lk 9:16—the miraculous feeding of the multitude); "praeclarum (calicem)" (Ps 22[23]:5); "mysterium fidei" (1 Tim 3:9).

Another indication of the biblical "simplicity" of the Narrative is the lack of rhythmic *clausulae* (see more on this topic below). This suggests that this part of the prayer did not undergo the same revision according to the rules of rhetoric as the other parts of the Canon. In fact, the only such reworking would seem to have been the replacement of the paratactic "respexit in caelum" in Ambrose's Narrative

[14] E. C. Ratcliff, "The Institution Narrative of the Roman Canon Missae: Its Beginning and Early Background", in *Liturgical Studies*, ed. A. H. Couratin and D. H. Tripp (London: SPCK, 1976), 51.

[15] Ibid.

by the ablative absolute "elevatis oculis in caelum" (with eyes raised to heaven).

The complex question of the Roman Institution Narrative's scriptural origins is advanced by Peter Burton's research on the Old Latin Gospels. Burton argues that "the Matthaean Passion narrative contains various peculiarities of translation that may derive from a liturgical text incorporated within the common source." [16] A significant case is the Latin rendering of the Greek ἐσθίω (eat): in the European witnesses of the *Vetus Latina*, the translation *manduco* is commonly found, while the African witnesses use both *manduco* and *edo* almost equally. It is remarkable that in the account of the Last Supper at Matthew 26:26, virtually all the manuscripts translate ἐσθίω with the same word: "ipsis autem cenantibus", or "cenantibus autem eis". Apparently, *cenare* is intended to imply a special kind of "eating", which justifies this unusual rendering.[17] Adducing a few more examples, Burton suggests, with some caution, that an earlier, separate liturgical version of the Last Supper account, or even of the whole Passion narrative, may have been incorporated into the Old Latin translation of Matthew's Gospel.

Burton concedes that his theory is hard to verify, especially because of the many variations between the manuscripts subsumed under title *Vetus Latina*. However, his argument confirms the ancient character of the Roman Institution Narrative, which, according to Ratcliff, has a particular theological significance:

> To such a liturgical tradition as this to which St. Cyprian is witness, an authentic scriptural, or rather Gospel, Institution

[16] P. Burton, *The Old Latin Gospels: A Study of Their Texts and Language* (Oxford: Oxford University Press, 2000), 34.

[17] Cf. ibid., 36–44 and 92.

Narrative is indispensable. For the function of the Narrative in the Canon is not merely to revive the memory of a significant historic event, or to provide a rationale for the celebration of the Eucharist, as the Greek Narratives do; its function is rather to make the significant historic event continuously present and operative. By means of the Narrative, therefore, the Church's *action* in the Eucharist is identified with, and becomes, the *action* of Christ in the Institution.[18]

Unde et Memores

The Anamnesis prayer following the Institution Narrative with the Consecration consists of one long sentence that connects the solemn memorial of Christ's saving actions (his Passion, Resurrection, and Ascension) with the offering of the eucharistic sacrifice. In order to express this act of offering, a characteristic chain of adjectives is used, which reads in Ambrose: "Offerimus tibi hanc immaculatum hostiam, rationabilem hostiam, incruentam hostiam, hunc panem sanctum et calicem vitae aeternae." The sequence of adjectives and the use of asyndeton are reminiscent of pagan Roman prayers.[19] In the Gregorian Canon, this phrase is modified to: "Offerimus praeclarae maiestati tuae de tuis donis ac datis

---

[18] Ratcliff, "Institution Narrative", 62.

[19] M. K. Lafferty, "Translating Faith from Greek to Latin: Romanitas and Christianitas in Late Fourth-Century Rome and Milan", *Journal of Early Christian Studies* 11 (2003): 48–49, cites a prayer attributed by Livy to Scipio as he sets out to invade Africa: "Make them come back home with me healthy and safe victors, having conquered the enemy, decorated with spoils, laden with booty, and making their triumph; give them the opportunity of taking vengeance on their enemies and foes" (salvos incolumesque victis perduellibus victores, spoliis decoratos, praeda onustos triumphantesque mecum domum reduces sistatis; inimicorum hostiumque ulciscendorum copiam faxitis); Livy, *Ab Urbe Condita* 29, 27, 2–4.

hostiam puram, hostiam sanctam, hostiam immaculatam, panem sanctum vitae aeternae et calicem salutis perpetuae" (We offer to your glorious majesty from the gifts that you have given us, this pure victim, this holy victim, this spotless victim, the holy Bread of eternal life and the Chalice of everlasting salvation). There are several other interesting features of revision in this section of the Canon: for instance, the simple "tibi" is replaced with "maiestati tuae" (your majesty). While this expression is often thought to derive from court style, Bernard Botte has pointed to the fact that *maiestas* is only rarely used as an imperial title. In the Old Latin Bible, *maiestas* (along with *claritas*, *gloria*, or *honor*) is one of the renderings for δόξα, which in turn is the Septuagint translation for the Hebrew *kabod*, the "glory" of the Lord.[20] Hence the phrase has a much stronger biblical pedigree than usually assumed. The phrase "de tuis donis ac datis"[21] has a parallel in the Anaphora of Saint John Chrysostom, in the anamnesis prayer after the Institution Narrative, "thine own of thine own [τὰ σὰ ἐκ τῶν σῶν] we offer unto thee on behalf of all and for all."[22] The older formula "hunc panem sanctum et calicem vitae aeternae" is replaced with the more balanced parallelism "panem sanctum vitae aeternae et calicem salutis perpetuae", thus creating a reference to Psalm 115:13: "calicem salutaris".[23]

---

[20] B. Botte, "Maiestas", in Botte and Mohrmann, *Ordinaire de la messe*, 111–13.

[21] The phrase appears to be inspired by 1 Chronicles 29:14: "tua sunt omnia et quae de manu tua accepimus dedimus tibi": *Biblia sacra iuxta Vulgatam versionem*, ed. R. Weber and R. Gryson, 4th ed. (Stuttgart: Deutsche Bibelgesellschaft, 1994), 585.

[22] Cf. Mohrmann, *Liturgical Latin*, 59.

[23] Note that Jerome, in his translation of the psalter *iuxta Hebraeos*, renders this passage as "calicem salutis": *Biblia sacra iuxta Vulgatam versionem*, 918–19.

Supra Quae

This prayer begins with yet another example of a simpler and more "popular" paratactic construction being exchanged for a more "formal" relative clause, which links one section of the Eucharistic Prayer to the preceding one: where Ambrose has "Et petimus et precamur ut hanc oblationem suscipias", the received text of the Canon reads "Supra quae propitio ac sereno vultu respicere digneris et accepta habere" (Be pleased to look upon them with serene and kindly countenance, and to accept them). The idea of God's "face" or "countenance", which expresses his loving and merciful attention toward men, is deeply rooted in Scripture (for example, Psalms 26[27]:8 and 23[24]:6). The precise wording of the Gregorian Canon "sereno vultu", however, seems to take up a literary expression that was common in classical Rome.[24]

The Ambrosian formula "et petimus et precamur" (we both ask and pray) is a fine example of a doubling of the verb with an alliteration, which is typical of pagan prayers, where formulae such as "do dedicoque" (I give and devote) occur frequently. The formula in Ambrose is in fact an elegant one if compared with the common "precor quaesoque" (I pray and beseech), which is well attested in Livy, because it introduces some variation in meaning between the two verbs.[25] There are examples of this stylistic feature in the Gregorian Canon as well, for instance, in the section *Te igitur*: "supplices rogamus ac petimus". This prayer formula,

---

[24] Botte and Mohrmann, *Ordinaire de la messe*, 82 b, note Horace, *Carmina* I, 29, 26, and Ovid, *Tristia* I, 5, 27.

[25] On "precor quaesoque", see F. Hickson, *Roman Prayer Language: Livy and the Aeneid of Virgil* (Stuttgart: Teubner, 1993), 49 and 77.

with its rhetorical density, is also known in Greek Eucharistic Prayers of the Alexandrian tradition.[26]

Prose Rhythm

A significant feature in the fully developed Roman Canon is its prose rhythm, or *cursus*. According to the classical tradition of rhetoric, rhythm was an important factor in the structure and beauty of a prose text. Aristotle says that prose should not be metrical, but at the same time it should not be unrhythmical, either. What is without rhythm is "unlimited" and, hence, not pleasing to the classical ear; Aristotle therefore stipulates that every part of the sentence should have a certain rhythm.[27] Cicero equally appreciates the function of rhythm in artistic prose, but he confines it to the most important parts of the colon, that is, the beginning and the end of a clause. In the Latin rhetorical tradition shaped by Cicero and Quintilian, the ending, or *clausula*, became the most important part of a sentence to be constructed according to rhythmical principles.[28] Rhythmic *clausulae* are used in the sermons and treatises of a number

[26] "δεόμεθα καὶ παρακαλοῦμεν" appears in the Strassburg Papyrus and in the Anaphora of Saint Mark in the long intercessory part that follows the Preface and leads to the *Sanctus*; A. Hänggi and I. Pahl, *Prex eucharistica*, vol. 1: *Textus e variis liturgiis antiquioribus selecti*, 3rd ed., Spicilegium Friburgense 12 (Fribourg: Universitätsverlag, 1998), 116, ll. 18–19, and 102, l. 27. For a discussion of rhetorical elements in Greek Anaphoras, see H. Engberding, "Die Kunstprosa des eucharistischen Hochgebetes der griechischen Gregoriusliturgie", in *Mullus: Festschrift Theodor Klauser*, Jahrbuch für Antike und Christentum, Ergänzungsband 1 (Münster: Aschendorff, 1964), 100–110.

[27] Aristotle, *Rhetoric* III, 8: 1408b21–1409a24.

[28] Cicero, *De oratore* III, 50, 192; Quintilian, *Institutio oratoria* IX, 4, 60–66.

of Church Fathers, among them Leo the Great and Augustine, who also discusses the use of *clausulae* in the fourth book of *De doctrina christiana*.[29]

It was quite natural that the use of the *clausulae*, or *cursus* in the terminology of the Middle Ages, is found in the public prayer of the Church, too. *Clausulae* are a stock feature of Roman liturgical composition from the late forth century to the middle of the seventh, especially in the variable prayers dating from this time.[30] Geoffrey Willis identified twenty-two rhythmical endings in the Gregorian Canon (see appendix 2, below, pp. 114–15). The list shows that the forming of *clausulae* was characteristic of the stylistic development of the Canon: there are seven in the central parts of the Gregorian version, compared to only one in the corresponding text cited by Ambrose. At the same time, the number of *clausulae* in the Gregorian Canon, a text of considerable length, is low compared with their frequency in the variable prayers. Hence, the conclusion can be drawn that the Canon was revised not long after its first appearance around the year 390 and before the formative period of the other parts of the rite, which would seem to commence in the fifth century.

This discussion of rhythmic *clausulae* is somewhat simplified, because it does not consider the quantity of syllables, on which classical meter is based. For the purposes of this study, the ictus (or metrical stress) of a line is taken to

---

[29] Augustine, *De doctrina christiana* IV, 115–17 and 147 (xx, 41, and xxvi, 56): ed. Green, 250 and 274; on the importance of prose rhythm in the Christian Latin *Kunstprosa*, see M. Marin, "La prosa d'arte cristiana latina", in *Il latino e i cristiani: Un bilancio all'inizio del terzo millennio*, ed. E. dal Covoloa and M. Sodi, Monumenta Studia Instrumenta Liturgica 17 (Vatican City: Libreria Editrice Vaticana, 2002), 29–37, with further bibliographical references.

[30] Haessly, *Rhetoric in the Sunday Collects*, 7–9.

coincide with the word accent. By the end of the fourth century, the quantitative distinction had largely disappeared from spoken language; the accentuated syllable, which was used to indicate a raising of pitch in the voice, became tonal, that is, it became a forceful stress of the accentuated syllable, as in modern languages. Thus, a new sort of rhythmical versification based on the number of syllables and the placing of accents began to appear; an early example is Augustine's so-called *Psalmus contra partem Donati*.[31]

In the Roman Canon, there are examples of the three common types of *clausulae*:

—*cursus planus* (even), with the accent on the second and the fifth syllables from the end: "órbe terrárum", "placátus accípias", "páce dispónas";

—*cursus tardus* (slow), with the accent on the third and the sixth syllables from the end: "damnatióne nos éripi", "salútis perpétuae";

—*cursus velox* (fast), with the accent on the second and seventh syllables from the end: "gloriósae ascensiónis", "grátia repleámur";

In addition to these three, there is the *cursus trispondaicus*, with three unaccented syllables between two accented ones: "grége numerári", "respícere dignéris".

In the prayer *Supplices te rogamus*, I have added the *clausula* "sánguinem sumpserímus", as suggested by Zoltán Rihmer, who argues that, according to late ancient grammarians, the stress would have been on the second syllable from the end,

[31] On this topic, see the study of G. Díaz Patri, "Poetry in the Latin Liturgy", in *The Genius of the Roman Liturgy: Historical Diversity and Spiritual Reach: Proceedings of the 2006 Oxford CIEL Colloquium*, ed. U.M. Lang (Chicago: Hillenbrand Books, 2010), 45–82.

not on the third, according to the Renaissance humanists who formed our understanding of Latin.[32] The two *clausulae* "sánguinem sumpserímus" and "grátia repleámur" would then form a neat parallelism at the end of the prayer, emphasizing the petition to enjoy the supernatural fruits of sacramental communion:

ut quotquot ex hac altaris participatione sacrosanctum Filii tui corpus et sánguinem sumpserímus
omni benedictione caelesti et grátia repleámur.

so that all of us who through this participation at the altar receive the most holy Body and Blood of your Son,
may be filled with every grace and heavenly blessing.

The Variable Prayers of the Mass

The variable prayers of the Roman rite are later in origin than the Eucharistic Prayer and may go back as far as the first half of the fifth century.[33] The prayers also known as "Collects" (a term that is not of Roman but of Gallican origin)[34] have a proper style that is quite distinct from the Canon of the Mass. The characteristics of this style are well established already in the earliest examples that have come down to us in the Verona manuscript, which is from the first quarter of the seventh century but contains material

[32] I owe this point to a discussion with Dr. Rihmer in Oxford in September 2006.

[33] For a useful overview of recent research in this field, see J. G. Leachman, "History of Collect Studies", in *Appreciating the Collect: An Irenic Methodology*, ed. J. G. Leachman and D. P. McCarthy, Liturgiam Aestimare: Appreciating the Liturgy 1 (Farnborough: Saint Michael's Abbey Press, 2008), 1–25.

[34] The history of the term *collecta* is traced by P. Regan, "The Collect in Context", in Leachman and McCarthy, *Appreciating the Collect*, 83–103.

that is dated variously from 400 to 560.[35] The Veronense (also known as "Leonine Sacramentary") was probably not used in public worship in the form in which it has come down to us but should be taken as a private compilation of Roman formularies of different age and authority.

The style of the early Roman Collects is terse, well balanced, and economical in its expression; each prayer is always a single sentence, even if the syntax can at times be complex. In fact, many of these Collects are considered literary masterpieces. In her study of the Sunday Collects of the *Missale Romanum*, where the oldest euchological material of the Roman rite is preserved, Mary Gonzaga Haessly distinguishes between a Protasis (Prelude), which is "the basis or background for the Petition", and an Apodosis (Theme), which "is, in general, the part of the Collect that expresses the purpose of the Prayer, or the goal toward which it gravitates".[36] The Protasis usually in some way anticipates the Petition of the prayer, which is in turn fulfilled in the Apodosis. Haessly also notes:

> Besides the general division of the Collect into Protasis (Prelude) and Apodosis (Theme), every Collect has three parts: the Address, the Petition, the Conclusion. In the Address God is invoked under various titles, and frequently the invocation is accompanied by a relative clause, which I have called Statement of Fact. This clause refers to the feast of the day, or to an attribute of God. . . . The Petition, usually expressed by an imperative, is sometimes strengthened by the word 'quaesumus', which I have called the Formula of Petition.[37]

---

[35] See C. Vogel, *Medieval Liturgy: An Introduction to the Sources*, trans. W. Storey and N. Rasmussen (Washington, D.C.: Pastoral Press, 1981), 38–45.

[36] Haessly, *Rhetoric in the Sunday Collects*, 13.

[37] Ibid., 14–15.

The Collect, in its mature form, ends with the conclusion "per Dominum nostrum Iesum Christum . . .", which is a profession of faith and an act of praise in honor of the Most Holy Trinity.

In its complete form, the Collect has the following structure:

1. an address to God, generally to the Father;
2. a relative or participial clause referring to some attribute of God or to one of his saving acts;
3. the petition, either in the imperative or in the subjunctive;
4. the reason or desired result for which the petition is made;
5. the conclusion.[38]

An example of this complete form is this Sunday Collect, already found in the Old Gelasian Sacramentary and used for the Eleventh Sunday after Pentecost (*Missale Romanum* 1570/1962) or the Twenty-Seventh Sunday *per annum* (*Missale Romanum* 1970/2008).[39] The prayer is remarkable for its literary beauty and theological richness:

1. Omnipotens sempiterne Deus,
2. qui abundantia pietatis tuae et merita supplicum excedis et vota,
3. effunde super nos misericordiam tuam,
4. ut dimittas quae consicentia metuit

[38] This structure is adapted from Willis, *History of Early Roman Liturgy*, 63–64; a similar, more detailed methodology for analyzing the prayers is presented by R. De Zan, "How to Interpret a Collect", in Leachman and McCarthy, *Appreciating the Collect*, 57–82.

[39] *Gelasianum*, 1201: ed. L. C. Mohlberg, *Liber Sacramentorum Romanae Aeclesiae Ordinis Anni Circuli*, Rerum Ecclesiasticarum Documenta, Series maior, Fontes IV, 3rd ed. (Rome: Herder, 1981); cf. *Corpus orationum*, ed. E. Moeller, J.-M. Clément, and B. Coppieters 't Wallant, 14 vols., CCSL 160 (Turnhout: Brepols, 1992–2004), no. 3887.

4. et adicias quod oratio non praesumit.
5. Per Dominum. . . .

1. Almighty, ever-living God,
2. who in the abundance of your kindness surpass the merits and the desires of those who entreat you,
3. pour out your mercy upon us:
4. to pardon what conscience dreads
4. and to give what prayer does not dare to ask.
5. Through our Lord. . . .[40]

This structure need not always be rigidly followed; some elements may be rearranged, duplicated, or omitted. For instance, in the following prayer, which is used in various ancient sacramentaries for the Third Sunday of Lent (also *Missale Romanum* 1570/1962),[41] there is no relative or participial clause after the address to God, and the reason or desired result of the petition is omitted:

1. Quaesumus, omnipotens Deus,
3. vota humilium respice
3. atque ad defensionem nostram dexteram tuae maiestatis extende.
5. Per Dominum. . . .

1. We beseech you, almighty God,
3. look upon the prayers of the lowly;

[40] English translation from the *Roman Missal* 2011.

[41] For instance, *Gellonense*, 389: ed. A. Dumas, *Liber Sacramentorum Gellonensis*, CCSL 159 (Turnhout: Brepols, 1981); *Gregorianum (Hadrianum)*, 229: ed. J. Deshusses, *Le Sacramentaire Grégorien: Ses principales formes d'après les plus anciens manuscrits*, vol. 1, 3rd ed. Spicilegium Friburgense 16 (Fribourg: Éditions Universitaires, 1992); Paduanum, 202: ed. L. C. Mohlberg and A. Baumstark, *Die älteste erreichbare Gestalt des Liber Sacramentorum anni circuli der römischen Kirche*, Liturgiegeschichtliche Quellen 11/12 (Münster: Aschendorff, 1927); see *Corpus orationum*, no. 4915a.

3. and for our defense stretch out the right hand of your majesty.
5. Through our Lord. . . .[42]

This simpler and more direct form is less frequently used for the Collect of the Mass but is found more often in the Prayer over the Offerings (Secret) and the Post-Communion Prayer.

The elements of the Collects may also be inversed and rearranged, as in the following prayer, which is found with slight variation in early sacramentaries.[43] It appears as the Prayer over the People for the Wednesday after the Fourth Sunday of Lent (*Missale Romanum* 1570/1962) or Saturday in the Second Week of Lent (*Missale Romanum* 1970/2008) and as the Collect of the Ninth Sunday after Pentecost (*Missale Romanum* 1570/1962):

3. Pateant aures misericordiae tuae,
1. Domine,
3. precibus supplicantium,
4. et ut desiderata consequantur,
3. fac eos, quae tibi placita sunt, postulare.
5. Per Dominum. . . .

3. May the ears of your mercy be open,
1. O Lord,
3. to the prayers of those who call upon you;

[42] The translation is from L. Pristas, "The Post-Vatican II Revision of the Lenten Collects", in *Ever Directed Towards the Lord: The Love of God in the Liturgy of the Eucharist Past, Present, and Hoped For*, ed. U. M. Lang (London: T&T Clark (Continuum), 2007), 77, who also offers a brief discussion of the prayer.

[43] It is used as a Sunday Collect (for example, *Gelasianum*, 1195) and as a Collect or Prayer over the People for weekdays in Lent (for example, *Paduanum*, 245), see *Corpus orationum*, no. 4145.

4. and that you may grant what they desire
3. have them ask what is pleasing to you.
5. Through our Lord. . . .[44]

Parallels have rightly been noted between the characteristic first and second element of the Collect, that is, the address to God followed by a relative clause, and pagan Roman prayers.[45] However, Mohrmann would seem correct in arguing that this structure simply reflects a general euchological form that is found in many religious traditions.[46] Anton Baumstark has already observed that in the early Roman Collects, the initial form of praise is linked with a prayer of petition, according to the supreme model of the Lord's Prayer: "Our Father, who art in heaven. . . ."[47] This structure naturally follows the model of the Jewish *berakah*, where a relative clause follows the invocation "Blessed are you, Lord our God. . . ."[48]

Mohrmann describes the style of the Collects as closer to the cultural and literary traditions of classical Rome and their vocabulary as farther removed from Sacred Scripture than the Canon and the Prefaces.[49] While this observation is generally correct, the biblical provenance of the Collects' vocabulary should not be overlooked; this is evident not so

[44] Translation from the *Roman Missal* 2011.

[45] For instance, Livy, *Ab Urbe Condita* 29, 27, 2–4: "Divi divaeque, qui maria terrasque colitis, vos precor quaesoque uti. . . ."

[46] Thus Mohrmann, *Liturgical Latin*, 67–68. Cf. the Egyptian and Assyrian prayers in *Preghiere dell'umanità*, ed. P. Miquel and M. Perrini, trans. P. Brognoli and M. Perrrini (Brescia: Queriniana, 1993), 30 and 37.

[47] See A. Baumstark, *Liturgie comparée: Principes et méthodes pour l'étude historique des liturgies chrétiennes*, 3rd ed., rev. by B. Botte, Collection Irénikon (Chevetogne: Éditions de Chevetogne, 1953), 73.

[48] Cf. the collection of Jewish liturgical texts in Hänggi and Pahl, *Prex eucharistica*, 1:5–57.

[49] See Mohrmann, *Ordinaire de la messe*, 44–47.

much from direct quotations (although there are some) as from general resonances and "plays" on scriptural words and concepts.[50] An example of this pattern can be found in the initial petition of the above-mentioned Collect that the ears of God's mercy be open to the prayers of those who call upon him. This striking anthropomorphism is typical of biblical expression; in the Old Testament, eyes, ears, arms, and so forth, are attributed to God.

The variable prayers of the Mass originated in a given period, and the statements and petitions formulated in them often reflect a particular moment in the history of the Roman Church. As Willis notes: "In such cases the Pope, or somebody under his instructions, might compose the variable prayers and the Preface of a Mass, which would be used on the occasion for which it was designed, and then filed in the papal chancery for possible use on later occasions. Collections of such propers or masses began to be made, and these were called *libelli sacramentorum*."[51] The Verona manuscript is precisely such a collection and not a sacramentary in the full sense, which would contain the proper texts of Masses for all, or most, Sundays and Holy Days.

As these early liturgical texts show similarities in style and content to writings of some Church Fathers, scholars have made an effort to infer their possible authors and to relate them to specific historical circumstances. To name a few examples: Frank Leslie Cross considers the literary

---

[50] See G. Moore, "The Vocabulary of the Collects: Retrieving a Biblical Heritage", in Leachman and McCarthy, *Appreciating the Collect*, 175–95, and A. A. R. Bastiaensen, "Die Bibel in den Gebetsformeln der lateinischen Kirche", in *The Impact of Scripture in Early Christianity*, ed. J. den Boeft and M. L. van Poll-van de Lisdonk, Supplements to Vigiliae Christianae 44 (Leiden, Boston, and Cologne: Brill, 1999), 39–57.

[51] G. G. Willis, "The Variable Prayers of the Roman Mass", in *Further Essays in Early Roman Liturgy*, 92.

parallels between the Veronense and the sermons of Pope Leo the Great, arguing that Leo actually uses phrases from older liturgical texts;[52] in a series of studies, Arthur Paul Lang explores the resemblances between euchological material in the Roman rite and the preaching of Pope Leo;[53] Antoine Chavasse identifies in the Veronense a number of Masses composed by Pope Gelasius (492–496) and by Pope Vigilius (537–555);[54] likewise, Bernard Capelle sees in the Veronense some Masses by Gelasius and some retouches made by the same pope;[55] Henry Ashworth holds that the Collects of Septuagesima, Sexagesima, and Quinquagesima

---

[52] F. L. Cross, "Pre-Leonine Elements in the Proper of the Roman Mass", *Journal of Theological Studies* 50 (1949): 191–97.

[53] A. P. Lang, *Leo der Grosse und die Texte des Altgelasianums mit Berücksichtigung des Sacramentarium Leonianum und des Sacramentarium Gregorianum* (Steyl: Steyler Verlagsbuchhandlung, 1957); "Leo der Große und die Dreifaltigkeitspräfation", *Sacris Erudiri* 9 (1957): 116–62; "Anklänge an liturgische Texte in Epiphaniesermonen Leos des Grossen", *Sacris Erudiri* 10 (1958): 43–126; "Leo der Grosse und die liturgischen Texte des Oktavtages von Epiphanie", *Sacris Erudiri* 11 (1960): 12–135; "Anklänge an Orationen der Ostervigil in Sermonen Leos des Grossen", *Sacris Erudiri* 13 (1962): 281–325; "Leo der Grosse und die liturgischen Gebetstexte des Epiphaniefestes", *Sacris Erudiri* 14 (1963): 3*–22*; "Anklänge an Orationen der Ostervigil in Sermonen Leos des Grossen", *Sacris Erudiri* 18 (1967–1968): 5–119; "Anklänge an eine Heilig Geist Oration in einem Sermo Leos des Grossen auf die Fastenzeit", *Sacris Erudiri* 23 (1978–1979): 143–70; "Anklänge an Orationen der Ostervigil in Sermonen Leos des Grossen", in *Sacris Erudiri* 27 (1984): 129–49; "Anklänge an Orationen der Ostervigil in Sermonen Leos des Grossen", *Sacris Erudiri* 28 (1985): 155–381.

[54] A. Chavasse, "Messes du pape Vigile (537–555) dans le sacramentaire léonien", *Ephemerides Liturgicae* 64 (1950): 161–213, and 66 (1952): 145–215.

[55] B. Capelle, "Messes du pape s. Gélase dans le sacramentaire de Vérone", "Retouches gélasiennes dans le sacramentaire de Vérone", and "L'oeuvre liturgique de s. Gélase", in Capelle, *Travaux liturgiques de doctrine et d'histoire*, vol. 2: *Histoire: La messe* (Louvain: Abbaye du Mont César, 1962), 79–105, 106–15, and 146–60; cf. also C. Coebergh, "S. Gélase Ier, auteur principal de plusieurs messes et prières du sacramentaire léonien", *Ephemerides Liturgicae* 65 (1951): 171–81.

Sundays were written by Saint Gregory the Great during the Lombard invasion at the beginning of his pontificate.[56]

While there are obvious parallels between Latin liturgical texts of late antiquity and the writings of Church Fathers of the same period, any attempt to identify the author or redactor of a particular prayer will remain in the realm of probability. In the case of a well-known preacher, such as Leo the Great, it is difficult to determine whether he cites a prayer that is already in use, whether he is the author of the prayer, or whether the prayer is formed later by putting together phrases and expressions from his preaching. It would appear even more questionable to define the precise historical circumstances of a prayer, because the ancient Roman Collects are usually very general in their content and would fit a variety of particular situations, especially in the turbulent period after the fall of the Western Empire.

I shall briefly discuss both the question of possible historical origins and the principles of rhetorical composition with the help of an example taken from early Roman tradition. This Collect is assigned by the Verona manuscript to the Vigil of Pentecost;[57] it is preceded by the rubric "For the fast of the fourth month" (*In ieiunio quarti mensis*), which is a reference to Zechariah 8:19 and would indicate

[56] H. Ashworth, "The Influence of the Lombard Invasions on the Gregorian Sacramentary", *Bulletin of the John Rylands Library, Manchester* 37 (1954): 305–27; also "The Liturgical Prayers of St Gregory the Great", *Traditio* 15 (1959): 107–61, and the earlier study by B. Capelle, "La main de S. Grégorie dans le sacramentaire grégorien", *Revue Bénédictine* 49 (1937): 13–28.

[57] Veronense, 207: ed. L.C. Mohlberg, *Sacramentarium Veronense* (*Cod. Bibl. Capit. Veron. LXXXV[80]*), Rerum Ecclesiasticarum Documenta, Series Maior, Fontes I, 3rd ed. (Rome: Herder, 1978). The prayer is found under the heading "X. Orationes pridie Penticosten" and under the subheading "II. Item alia", which refers to the previous "I. In Pentecosten ascendentibus a fonte".

the Ember Days after Pentecost. While this indication is not entirely clear, it would also suggest that the same prayer is made on both occasions. This is at least so in the later *Gelasianum Vetus*, where the same Collect is used on the Vigil of Pentecost and on the Wednesday of the fast of the fourth month.[58] The prayer was transferred to Wednesday in Quinquagesima, as a number of ancient sacramentaries testify,[59] and this may have been done in the seventh century when the beginning of the Lenten season was moved to this day, later known as Ash Wednesday. Subsequently, the Collect was associated with the blessing and imposition of ashes and remained so in the *Missale Romanum* of 1570/1962, where it is the final prayer of this rite. In the *Missale Romanum* of 1970/2008, it is the opening Collect of the Mass of Ash Wednesday.[60] It is worth noting the stability of the text, which shows very few and insignificant variants in the manuscript tradition:

Concede nobis, Domine,
praesidia militiae christianae sanctis inchoare ieiuniis;
ut contra spirituales nequitias pugnaturi,
continentiae muniamur auxiliis.

Grant, O Lord, that we may begin with holy fasting
this campaign of Christian service,
so that as we take up battle against spiritual evils,
we may be armed with weapons of self-restraint.[61]

---

[58] *Gelasianum* LXXVIII, 631, and LXXXIII, 654; see *Corpus orationum*, no. 673A.

[59] *Gregorianum (Hadrianum)*, 153; *Paduanum*, 127; see *Corpus orationum*, no. 673B.

[60] Cf. A. Ward, "The Orations for Ash Wednesday in the Present Roman Missal", *Notitiae* 44 (2007): 45–49.

[61] English translation from the *Roman Missal* 2011.

The prayer is particularly interesting from a historical point of view because it bears a striking resemblance to a passage from Leo the Great's *Sermo* 78.[62] These evident literary parallels have been explained in different ways: Camille Callewaert sees Leo as the author of these prayers,[63] whereas Frank Leslie Cross argues that the fifth-century pope in his sermon quotes from liturgical texts already in use.[64] This would mean that some of the prayers of the Veronense may go back to the early decades of the fifth century. While the question cannot be determined with absolute certainty, Cross makes a good case for the Collect under discussion here, which is quoted almost in its entirety by Leo.

The prayer begins straightaway with the petition in the imperative ("Grant us"), and the address that follows is the simple form, without a relative clause ("O Lord"). The immediacy of the prayer gives it a serious, if not sharp, tone that corresponds with its stark theme: the idea of *militia christiana*, the Christian campaign or, indeed, warfare against spiritual wickedness.[65] This idea of the Christian life is greatly indebted to Saint Paul: "We are not contending against flesh and blood, but . . . against the spiritual hosts of wickedness [*spiritualia nequitia*, Vg.] in heavenly places" (Eph 6:12). Since the prayer is made on the day before Pentecost, at the conclusion of the Easter Season, the Apostle's exhortation may also be pertinent: "Let us, therefore, celebrate the festival, not with the old leaven, the leaven of malice and evil

---

[62] Leo the Great, *Sermo* 78, 2: PL 54:416.

[63] C. Callewaert, *S. Léon le Grand et les textes du Léonien* (extract from *Sacris Erudiri* I, 1948) (Bruges: Beyart; La Haye: Nijhoff, 1948), esp. 56–59.

[64] Cross, *Pre-Leonine Elements*.

[65] Cf. M. P. Ellebracht, *Remarks on the Vocabulary of the Ancient Orations in the Missale Romanum*, 2nd ed., Latinitas Christianorum Primaeva 18 (Nijmegen and Utrecht: Dekker & Van de Vegt, 1966), 173–78.

[*nequitiae*, Vg.], but with the unleavened bread of sincerity and truth" (1 Cor 5:8). The whole prayer presents a robust view of the Christian life and uses strong, military connotations: *praesidium*, which is commonly used in prayers to signify divine help or protection, is employed here in its military sense as defenses, protections, posts, or fortifications; *inchoare* means to lay the foundation of something or simply to begin. Thus the praying community (note the first person plural throughout) asks the Lord to enable it to "to lay the foundation of the protections of Christian warfare with holy fasts".

The petition of the prayer is amplified in the form of a purpose clause: we ask that we who are about to engage with (*pugnare*) spiritual evils may be strengthened (*munire*—another term with military connotations: to build a wall around, to defend, to secure) by aids or weapons (*auxilia*, also evoking auxiliary troops) of continence or self-restraint. Again this invokes a passage from Saint Paul: "the weapons of our warfare [*arma militiae nostrae*, Vg.] are not worldly" (2 Cor 10:4).[66] The second and fourth line of the prayer have an unusual word order because of the rhetorical device known as hyperbaton: the noun is separated from the modifying adjective, and respectively from the explicative genitive, by a verb. Thus a particular emphasis on the last word of each line is created: the *aids* of the Christian campaign consist in *fasting*. The parallel between the conclusion of the prayer and the main petition is highlighted not only by the rhyme, but also through the *cursus tardus* found at the end of both cola: *inchoáre ieiúniis*—*muniámur auxíliis*.

[66] Cf. A. Blaise, *Le vocabulaire latin des principaux thèmes liturgiques*, rev. A. Dumas (Turnhout: Brepols, 1966), 575 (§ 440).

As already indicated, the Collect was originally used on the Vigil of Pentecost, a solemn day of preparation for the great feast and the second most important date for conferring the sacrament of baptism in the Roman Church, after the Easter Vigil. In fact, the Collect has strong baptismal resonances. Taking their cue from the Second Letter to Timothy, early Christian writers saw in the sacraments of initiation the beginning of a *militia Christiana*: the newly baptized has become a "soldier of Christ" (2 Tim 2:3–4). This also recalls the use of the Latin word *sacramentum* as a technical military term for the oath of obedience and loyalty that a soldier must pledge upon entering the Roman army. For the early Christians, the baptismal promises, where the candidates reject Satan and profess their faith in God, were like an oath of fidelity to Christ and his Church.[67]

The Collect was also assigned to the Ember Wednesday after Pentecost. This is fitting, because the Ember Days are dedicated in a special way to prayer and fasting or abstinence and thus call to practice the "spiritual warfare" of which the Collect speaks. The theme of the prayer evidently made it ideal for the beginning of the holy season of Lent, and it has remained in use on Ash Wednesday ever since, though no longer in connection with the blessing and imposition of ashes in the *Missale Romanum* of 1970/2008.

The Prefaces

It is a characteristic of Western liturgies for the Preface, originally considered the beginning of the Eucharistic Prayer,

---

[67] Cf. D. G. van Slyke, "The Changing Meanings of *sacramentum*: Historical Sketches", *Antiphon* 11 (2007): 252–53 (on Tertullian).

to vary according to the liturgical season or feast. Its general theme is praise and thanksgiving for the divine economy of salvation and so naturally leads to the heart of the eucharistic liturgy. The tone of the Preface is more lyrical than the rest of the Canon and corresponds with the celebrant's call to the people: "Lift up your hearts (*Sursum corda*)". The great number of Prefaces in the ancient Roman sources suggests that improvisation and new composition prevailed here much longer than in the rest of the Canon. The Verona manuscript has a proper Preface for every Mass (267 altogether); the Old Gelasian limits their number to fifty-four, while the (Frankish Gelasian) Sacramentary of Saint Gall still has 186. Subsequently, however, the number of Prefaces was significantly reduced, and the copy of the Gregorian sacramentary sent by Pope Hadrian I to Charlemagne in the late eighth century (the *Hadrianum*) has only fourteen. The *Missale Romanum* of 1570 has eleven Prefaces, to which several were added in the twentieth century. The reform of the liturgy after the Second Vatican Council greatly expanded the corpus of Prefaces to eighty-one in the *Missale Romanum* of 1970, to which more were added in the second and third typical editions.[68]

As Josef Andreas Jungmann notes,[69] there were good reasons for the pruning of Prefaces: many of the texts in the

[68] See A. Ward and C. Johnson, eds., *The Prefaces of the Roman Missal: A Source Compendium with Concordance and Indices* (Rome: Tipografia Poliglotta Vaticana, 1989). The new Prefaces are not simply taken from ancient sacramentaries but are either centonizations, with phrases from various liturgical sources being woven together, liturgical transpositions of biblical, patristic, and Vatican II texts, or entirely new compositions. See L. Pristas, "The Orations of the Vatican II Missals: Policies for Revision", *Communio* (*US*) 30 (2003): 636–38.

[69] J. A. Jungmann, *Missarum Sollemnia: Eine genetische Erklärung der römischen Messe*, 2 vols., 5th ed. (Vienna: Herder, 1962), 2:145–61.

Veronense are exuberant in style and content and introduce idiosyncratic ideas that can detract from the tenor of this solemn opening of the Eucharistic Prayer. For instance, some of them dwell excessively on the lives of martyrs and so become almost a panegyric for a Christian hero. The purification that is evident in the Gregorian tradition was perhaps too drastic, but it was necessary in order to retain the distinctive Preface style.

The introductory dialogue, which in some form or other is common to most liturgical traditions, reads in its fully developed Roman form:

> Dominus vobiscum.
> Et cum spiritu tuo.
>
> Sursum corda.
> Habemus ad Dominum.
>
> Gratias agamus Domino Deo nostro.
> Dignum est iustum est.
>
> The Lord be with you.
> And with your spirit.
>
> Lift up your hearts.
> We lift them up to the Lord.
>
> Let us give thanks to the Lord our God.
> It is right and just.

Elements of this dialogue can be traced back to the third century: Cyprian of Carthage refers to the priest's exhortation "Sursum corda" and the people's response "Habemus ad Dominum."[70] The *Traditio Apostolica* has the entire

---

[70] Cyprian of Carthage, *De dominica oratione*, 31: CSEL 3:289.

Roman introductory dialogue, except for the addition "Deo nostro" to the celebrant's last exhortation.[71] While this text can no longer be taken simply as a witness to Roman liturgical practice in the third century, it is nonetheless a testimony to the antiquity of the introductory dialogue.

The dialogue itself is thoroughly biblical and follows Jewish prayers of thanksgiving.[72] The people's final response, "Dignum est iustum", belongs to the kind of acclamation that was a common feature of popular assemblies in the ancient world. Such acclamations confirmed an important decision or election, including that of a Roman emperor.[73] Later they were also used to approve the election of a bishop.[74]

This response is then taken up by the celebrant in the first part of the Preface itself (also known by its technical term "protocol"):

> Vere dignum et iustum est, aequum et salutare,
> nos tibi semper et ubique gratias agere:
> Domine, sancte Pater, omnipotens aeterne Deus:
> per Christum Dominum nostrum.

---

[71] *Traditio apostolica* 4, 3: ed. P. F. Bradshaw, M. E. Johnson, and L. E. Philips, *The Apostolic Tradition: A Commentary*, Hermeneia (Minneapolis, Minn.: Fortress Press, 2002), 38.

[72] Cf. Ruth 2:4, Luke 1:24, 2 Timothy 4:22, Colossians 3:1, Lamentations 3:41, 1 Thessalonians 1:2. A full list of biblical references is compiled by L. Eizenhöfer, *Canon Missae romanae: Pars altera: Textus propinqui*, Rerum Ecclesiasticarum Documenta, Series minor, Subsidia studiorum 7 (Rome: Herder, 1966), 21–24.

[73] "Aequm est, iustum est"; cf. the references in Eizenhöfer, *Canon Missae romanae*, 25.

[74] See Jungmann, *Missarum Sollemnia*, 2:139–40, who also points to a similar response in Jewish morning prayer.

It is truly right and just, our duty and our salvation,
always and everywhere to give you thanks,
Lord, holy Father, almighty and eternal God,
through Christ our Lord.

The rhetorical character of the Preface is expressed, for instance, in the threefold address to God. Here the shorter invocation precedes the longer, and so a memorable climax is achieved: "Lord, holy Father, almighty and eternal God".[75] While there can be variations in the phrasing, the protocol always follows this pattern: the celebrant, in the name of the people present and indeed of all the Church, proclaims that thanksgiving is due to God the Father through Jesus Christ.

The central part (or "embolism") provides the motive why the Church renders praise and thanks to God on this day and therefore varies according to the liturgical season or feast that is celebrated. As an example, I have chosen the first of the two Prefaces of the Nativity in *Missale Romanum* 1970/2008 (Preface of the Nativity in *Missale Romanum* 1570/1962):

Quia per incarnati Verbi mysterium
nova mentis nostrae oculis lux tuae claritatis infulsit:
ut dum visibiliter Deum cognoscimus
per hunc in invisibilium amorem rapiamur.

For in the mystery of the Word made flesh
a new light of your glory has shone upon the eyes
of our mind,

[75] In the *Missale Romanum* of 1570 and its subsequent editions, this was printed as "Domine sancte, Pater omnipotens, aeterne Deus". However, it has been shown conclusively that this punctuation is not correct, and so this has been changed in the *editio typica* of 1962; cf. C. Mohrmann, "Problèmes de ponctuation dans le préface", in Botte and Mohrmann, *Ordinaire de la messe*, 105.

so that as we recognize in him God made visible,
we may be caught up through him in love of things
invisible.[76]

This ancient Preface for Christmas[77] is a sublime expression of the human birth of the Son of God that is celebrated on one of the most solemn days of the liturgical year. The text obviously draws on the Gospel of John, especially on its prologue (1:1–14) and more generally on the Johannine theology presenting Christ as the light of the world. There is also a clear echo of the angel's apparition to the shepherds, announcing the birth of the Savior.[78] The themes of the Preface resonate particularly in the writings of Gregory the Great.[79]

The word *mysterium* has a wide-ranging meaning in liturgical texts and is found frequently in prayers for the celebration of the Nativity. When the first line of this passage evokes the "mystery of the incarnate Word", it employs the term to speak of divine revelation in Jesus Christ, much in the same way as Saint Paul uses μυστήριον (for instance, in Romans 16:25). This corresponds with the verb *cognoscere* in the third line, which clearly goes beyond intellectual

---

[76] English translation from the *Roman Missal* 2011.

[77] *Gregorianum (Hadrianum)*, 38 and 51; *Paduanum*, 6; cf. *Corpus praefationum*, ed. E. Moeller, 4 vols. CCSL 161 (Turnhout: Brepols, 1980–1981), no. 1322.

[78] Cf. the Vulgate version of Luke 2:9: "et claritas Dei circumfulsit illos" (and the glory of the Lord shone around them).

[79] Gregory the Great, *In Ezech* II, I, 15: SC 360:80: "Redemptor itaque noster, pro nobis misericorditer *incarnatus*, ante humanos *oculos* quasi in porta stetit, quia et per humanitatem *uisibilis* apparuit, et sese *inuisibilem* in diuinitate seruavit"; cf. *Moralia in Iob* XVIII, LI, 83: CCSL 143:946, and also Fulgentius of Ruspe, *Ad Trasimundum* 2, 6: PL 65:252B. For a full list of these biblical and patristic references, see Ward and Johnson, *Prefaces of the Roman Missal*, 72–74.

knowledge and includes "the idea of a real, effective experience of salvation".[80] The first and the third line are composed in such a way that they are related to each other by the same rhythmical ending (*cursus tardus*: "Vérbi mystérium—Déum cognóscimus").[81]

The theme of light, which suffuses the euchological texts for Christmas in the *Missale Romanum*, is greatly elaborated in the second line: the noun *lux* is separated from its modifying adjective by three words. By means of this hyperbaton and of the prominent position of *nova* at the beginning of the line, attention is drawn to the newness, in general, of Christian revelation and, in particular, of Christ's Nativity, which renews the whole world and liberates it from sin.[82] The apposition *tuae claritatis* can be construed as a genitive of identity or of inherence: the two words have approximately the same meaning. In Latin Bible versions, *claritas* is one of the possible translations for the Hebrew *kabod* and the Greek δόξα, that is, the manifestation

---

[80] Ellebracht, *Remarks on the Vocabulary*, 70; cf. 67–71.

[81] The second line and fourth line have different rhythmical endings: "claritátis infúlsit" (*cursus planus*) and "amórem rapiámur" (*cursus trispondiacus*).

[82] This is another frequent theme in Christmas prayers; cf. Ellebracht, *Remarks on the Vocabulary*, 24–25, and Blaise, *Vocabulaire latin*, 314 (§ 180). See, for instance, the striking phrase "Unigeniti tui nova per carnem nativitas" in the Collect for the Sixth Day within the Octave of the Nativity in *Missale Romanum* 1970/2008 (in *Missale Romanum* 1570/1962, this is the Collect for the *Missa in die* on Christmas Day):

> Grant, we pray, almighty God,
> that the newness of the Nativity in the flesh
> of your Only Begotten Son may set us free,
> for ancient servitude holds us bound
> beneath the yoke of sin.

English translation from *Roman Missal* 2011.

of God's glory,[83] which is now radiating in the newborn Christ child for those who look upon him with the eyes of faith.

The third line, with a subordinate clause in the indicative, explains the effect of the Incarnation, whereas the fourth line goes on to express the desired result with the subjunctive; in a very literal translation: "so that we, while we know God visibly, may be caught up into love[84] of things invisible". The verb *rapiare*, translating the Greek ἁρπάζειν, is adduced several times in the New Testament when a person is transported (in spirit or even physically) into the sphere of God. Thus "the Spirit of the Lord caught up" the Deacon Philip, after he had baptized the Ethiopian eunuch (Acts 8:39). The Apostle Paul speaks of being "caught up to the third heaven" in his own description of his mystical experience (1 Cor 12:2, 4).[85] Resonating with these scriptural passages, the embolism closes with a poetic invocation of enjoying eternal happiness, "what no eye has seen . . . what God has prepared for those who love him" (1 Cor 2:9; cf. Is 64:4).[86]

---

[83] For instance, in the sanctuary of the desert (Ex 40:33–35) and in the Temple of Jerusalem (1 Kings 8:11).

[84] There is an ancient variant at this point: *Paduanum*, 6, reads "invisibilium amore" instead of "in invisibilium amorem", thus saying that we "may be caught up *by* love of things invisible".

[85] See also 1 Thessalonians 4:17 and Revelation 12:5.

[86] The Post-Communion Prayer for the feast of the Ascension in *Missale Romanum* 1570/1962 (also found in Veronense, 172, with the variation of *celebrando* for *sumenda*) uses the same antithesis between invisible and visible when speaking of the grace that is given when the sacrament is received.

> Praesta nobis, quaesumus,
> omnipotens et misericors Deus:
> ut, quae visibilibus mysteriis sumenda percepimus,
> invisibili consequamur effectu.

Et ideo cum Angelis et Archangelis,
cum Thronis et Dominationibus,
cumque omni militia caelestis exercitus,
hymnum gloriae tuae canimus, sine fine dicentes:

And so, with Angels and Archangels,
with Thrones and Dominions,
and with all the hosts and Powers of heaven,
we sing the hymn of your glory
as without end we acclaim:

The concluding part (or "eschatocol") invokes the continuous praise rendered by the angels and saints to God in heaven and invites the earthly community to join in it, thus providing the transition to the *Sanctus*. A characteristic feature of many Prefaces is the reference to the choirs of angels, which developed from the Church Fathers' exegesis of Holy Scripture (for example, Gen 3:24, Ezek 28:14–16, Is 6: 2–3, Eph 1:21, and Col 1:16). Thus, a fittingly solemn prelude to the great acclamation of the thrice-holy God is provided.

* * *

The liturgical texts that have been analyzed in this chapter display a distinctive prayer style that is both Roman and Christian. The Canon and the variable texts of the Mass

---

Grant us, we pray,
almighty and merciful God,
that what we have received in invisible mysteries
may profit us by its invisible effect.

It may therefore not be too farfetched to see in the Preface of the Nativity also an allusion to the Most Holy Eucharist, which anticipates that eternal beatitude. This would no doubt have been Saint Thomas Aquinas' reason for choosing this Preface when he composed the Mass of the feast of Corpus Christ (see below, chap. 5, p. 149).

draw on the style of pagan prayer, including its juridical elements, but their vocabulary and content are distinctively Christian, indeed, biblical. Their diction has Roman *gravitas* and avoids the exuberance of the Eastern Christian prayer style, which is also found in the Gallican tradition. Mohrmann sees in these early Roman prayers the fortuitous combination of a renewal of language, inspired by the newness of Christian revelation, and a stylistic traditionalism that was firmly imbedded in the Roman world. The formation of this sacred language was part of a comprehensive effort to evangelize classical culture.

APPENDIX I

Ambrose of Milan, *De sacramentis*[1]	***Canon Romanus***[2]
Fac nobis hanc oblationem scriptam, rationabilem, acceptabilem, quod est figura corporis et sanguinis Domini nostri Iesu Christi.	Quam oblationem tu, Deus in omnibus, quaesumus, benedictam, adscriptam, ratam, rationabilem acceptabilemque facere digneris, ut nobis corpus et sanguis fiat dilectissimi Filii tui Domini Dei nostri Iesu Christi.
Qui pridie quam pateretur, in sanctis manibus suis accepit panem, respexit ad caelum, ad te, sancte Pater omnipotens aeterne Deus, gratias agens benedixit, fregit, fractumque apostolis et discipulis suis tradidit dicens: Accipite et edite ex hoc omnes; hoc est enim corpus meum, quod pro multis confringetur.	Qui pridie quam pateretur accepit panem in sanctas ac venerabiles manus suas elevatis oculis in caelum ad te Deum Patrem suum omnipotentem tibi gratias agens benedixit, fregit, dedit discipulis suis dicens: Accipite et manducate ex hoc omnes. Hoc est enim corpus meum. Simili modo, posteaquam

[1] Hänggi and Pahl, *Prex Eucharistia* 1:421–22.

[2] Ibid., 433–35.

Similiter etiam calicem, postquam cenatum est, pridie quam pateretur, accepit, respexit ad caelum, ad te, sancte Pater omnipotens aeterne Deus, gratias agens benedixit, apostolis et discipulis suis tradidit dicens: Accipite et bibite ex hoc omnes ; hic est enim sanguis meus. Quotienscumque hoc feceritis, totiens commemorationem mei facietis, donec iterum adveniam.

cenatum est, accipiens et hunc praeclarum calicem in sanctas ac venerabiles manus suas, item tibi gratias agens benedixit, dedit discipulis suis dicens: Accipite et bibite ex eo omnes. Hic est enim calix sanguinis mei, novi et aeterni testamenti, mysterium fidei, qui pro vobis et pro multis effundetur in remissionem peccatorum. Haec quotiescumque feceritis, in mei memoriam facietis.

Ergo memores gloriosissimae eius passionis et ab inferis resurrectionis et in caelum ascensionis offerimus tibi hanc inmaculatam hostiam, rationabilem hostiam, incruentam hostiam, hunc panem sanctum et calicem vitae aeternae.

Unde et memores sumus, Domine, nos tui servi sed et plebs tua sancta Christi Filii tui Domini Dei nostri tam beatae passionis nec non et ab inferis resurrectionis sed et in caelos gloriosae ascensionis offerimus praeclarae maiestati tuae de tuis donis ac datis hostiam puram, hostiam sanctam, hostiam immaculatam, panem sanctum vitae aeterna et calicem salutis perpetuae.

Et petimus et precamur, uti hanc oblationem suscipias in sublime altare tuum per manus angelorum tuorum, sicut suscipere dignatus es munera pueri tui iusti Abel et sacrificium patriarchae nostri Abrahae et quod tibi obtulit summus sacerdos Melchisedech.

Supra quae propitio ac sereno vultu respicere digneris et accepta habere, sicuti accepta habere dignatus es munera pueri tui iusti Abel et sacrificium patriarchae nostri Abrahae et quod tibi obtulit summus sacerdos tuus Melchisedech, sanctum sacrificium, immaculatam hostiam. Supplices te rogamus, omnipotens Deus, iube haec perferri per manus angeli tui in sublime altare tuum in conspectu divinae maiestatis tuae, ut quotquot ex hac altaris participatione sacrosanctum Filii tui corpus et sanguinem sumpserimus, omni benedictione caelesti et gratia repleamur per Christum Dominum nostrum.

APPENDIX 2

Rhythmic Clausulae in the Roman Canon[1]

Te igitur	
rogámus et pétimus	tardus
régere dignéris	trispondaicus
órbe terrárum	planus
Memento, Domine	
nóta devótio	tardus
Communicantes	
sanctórum tuórum	planus
precibúsque concédas	planus
muniámur auxílio	tardus
Hanc igitur	
familíae túae	planus
placátus accípias	planus
páce dispónas	planus
damnatióne nos éripi	tardus
grége numerári	trispondaicus
Quam oblationem	
Déus in ómnibus	tardus
fácere dignéris	trispondaicus

[1] Willis, *History of Early Roman Liturgy*, 33–34.

Qui pridie

– none –

Unde et memores

plébs tua sáncta	planus
glorióśae ascensiónis	velox
salútis perpétuae	tardus

Supra quae

respícere dignéris	trispondaicus

Supplices te rogamus

[sánguinem sumpserímus	velox]
grátia repleámur	velox

Memento etiam, Domine

indúlgeas deprecámur	uelox

Nobis quoque peccatoribus

donáre dignéris	planus
largítor admítte	planus

IV

FROM LATE ANTIQUITY TO THE MIDDLE AGES

A Period of Decadence?

Students of liturgical Latin, such as Christine Mohrmann, used to concentrate on what may be called the "classical" period of formation of the Roman rite from the fourth to the seventh century. Recently, more attention has been devoted to liturgical texts from a later period and to those originating, not from Rome, but from Gaul, Spain, and other parts of the Latin Church.[1] Els Rose has published a substantial work on liturgical Latin in the *Missale Gothicum*, along with her critical edition of this late seventh-century witness to the Gallican tradition.[2] While the merits of this research are beyond doubt, Rose uses the opportunity to

[1] For the Visigothic tradition, see, for instance, R. Wright, *Late Latin and Early Romance in Spain and Carolingian France*, ARCA 8 (Liverpool: Francis Cairns, 1982), 73–78; M. C. Díaz y Díaz, "El latín de la liturgia hispánica: Notas introductorias", in *Estudios sobre la liturgia mozárabe*, ed. J. Rivera Recio (Toledo: Diputación Provincial, 1965), 55–87.

[2] H. G. E. Rose, ed., *Missale gothicum e codice Vaticano Reginensi latino 317 editum*, CCSL 159D (Turnhout: Brepols, 2005); see also "Liturgical Latin in the Missale Gothicum (Vat. Reg. Lat. 317): A Reconsideration of Christine Mohrmann's approach", *Sacris Erudiri* 42 (2003): 97–121.

offer a harsh critique of Mohrmann's approach. She charges Mohrmann with promoting a "one-sided view of liturgical Latin [that is, a hieratic, highly stylized language with hardly any popular features]", because she confined her interpretation "to the liturgical texts of the *Patres* and the liturgy of the church of Rome, choosing her examples from these undoubtedly rich but restricted treasuries", passing over other traditions, such as the Gallican or Visigothic ones. Thus Mohrmann is said to present "an opinion on liturgical Latin based on a select corpus of sources but presented as a general view on the subject".[3]

In the first chapter of this book, I have discussed Mohrmann's concept of Christian Latin and have evaluated the criticism made by a number of scholars. Despite some shortcomings in her methodology, her work as a whole is not discredited or invalid. Mohrmann was obviously aware of non-Roman Latin liturgical sources,[4] but she chose as the scope of her studies the characteristically *Roman* prayer style, which liturgical scholars before her, such as Edmund Bishop,[5] had identified. This approach can and should be

---

[3] E. Rose, "Liturgical Latin in the Bobbio Missal", in *The Bobbio Missal: Liturgy and Religious Culture in Merovingian Gaul*, ed. Y. Hen and R. Meens, Cambridge Studies in Palaeography and Codicology (Cambridge: Cambridge University Press, 2004), 70.

[4] Cf. C. Mohrmann, "Quelques observations sur l'évolution stylistique du Canon de la Messe romain", in *Études sur le latin des chrétiens*, 4 vols., Storia e letteratura 65, 87, 103, 143 (Rome: Edizioni di Storia e Letteratura, 1961–1977), 3:235, n. 21.

[5] E. Bishop, "The Genius of the Roman Rite", in *Liturgica Historica* (Oxford: Clarendon Press, 1918), 1–19. Bishop's assessment of the distinctive Roman and Gallican features is generally correct, even if one need not follow the value judgment that is implied in his comparison; cf. P. Bradshaw, "The Genius of the Roman Rite Revisited", in *Ever Directed Towards the Lord: The Love of God in the Liturgy Past, Present, and Hoped For*, ed. U.M. Lang (London: T&T Clark, 2007), 49–61.

enlarged, and Rose's research, leaving aside unnecessary polemics, serves this purpose.

In her study of the *Bobbio Missal*, an important source for the Gallican tradition dating from the turn of the eighth century, Rose takes issue even with Robert Coleman, whose assessment of Mohrmann has been presented in the first chapter of this book, because he considers non-Roman liturgical sources of the seventh and eighth centuries as evidence of extensive vulgarization. As an example, Coleman observes that the Roman Canon appears in the *Bobbio Missal* in a truncated form that obscures its meaning. For instance, the phrase "intra quorum nos consortium non aestimator meriti sed ueniae, quaesumus, largitor admitte" (admit us, we beseech you, into their company, not weighing our merits, but granting us your pardon) becomes "intra quorum nos consorcio non stimator meritis sed ueniam quesomus largitur admitte." These modifications could be interpreted as orthographic peculiarities that would be typical of a period of transition from Latin to the Romance vernaculars. Nonetheless, Coleman, who speaks of a "garbled form", notes that "in a religion where departures from the prescribed form of words could raise doubts about the validity of the rites enacted by them, the motivation to restore was strong."[6] I cannot see how one could reject this conclusion.

Rose herself provides several examples of how the *Bobbio Missal* radically shortens prayers of the *Missale Gothicum* to the point that their grammar becomes confused and their contents can be understood only with difficulty.[7] She observes that, in some cases, "the scissor and paste work of the

[6] R. Coleman, "Vulgar Latin and the Diversity of Christian Latin", in *Actes du 1er Colloque international sur le latin vulgaire et tardif (Pécs, 2–5 septembre 1985)*, ed. J. Herman (Tübingen: Niemeyer, 1987), 47.

[7] See Rose, "Liturgical Latin in the Bobbio Missal", 71–76.

compiler of the Bobbio Missal has led to grammatically incorrect and incomprehensible texts."[8] Such phenomena would appear to confirm the decay of Latin literary culture in the Merovingian period, which prompted the efforts of churchmen and scholars under Charlemagne to purify and standardize liturgical books. The Carolingian *renovatio* restored the classical forms of liturgical Latin; however, by doing so, at the same time it created a greater distance between the language of the liturgy and the developing vernacular of the people.[9]

The Carolingian reforms of the educational system not only restored the classical standards of morphology and syntax in written Latin. The philologist Roger Wright maintains that the most significant change of the Carolingian age was the adoption of a standard spoken form of Latin, still employed today, which is based "on the phonographic assumption, that every written letter of the standard spelling should be given a regular sound".[10] This manner of pronunciation was already in use among Anglo-Saxon and Germanic scholars, such as Alcuin of York and Hrabanus Maurus, who were not native speakers. However, it was foreign to those who still spoke Latin as their native language in those parts of Europe that would subsequently

---

[8] Ibid., 72.

[9] Cf. E. Auerbach, *Literatursprache und Publikum in der lateinischen Spätantike und im Mittelalter* (Bern: Francke, 1958), 88 and 197.

[10] R. Wright, *A Sociophilological Study of Late Latin*, Utrecht Studies in Medieval Literacy 10 (Turnhout: Brepols, 2002), 347. This volume contains papers published in various places, some of them revised; cf. also his *Late Latin and Early Romance in Spain and Carolingian France*. Wright makes frequent reference to M. Banniard, *Viva voce: communication écrite et communication orale du IVe au IXe siècle en occident latin*, Collection des études augustiniennes: Série Moyen-âge et temps modernes 25 (Paris: Institut des études augustiniennes, 1992).

develop as the Romance-speaking world. This area was still a "monolingual speech community" in the early eighth century, despite local and sociolinguistic variations within the one language.[11] The standard pronunciation of Latin that was promoted effectively by the Carolingian scholars would have sounded artificial to native speakers, who in different regions assigned different sounds to the same written letter of a word. The new system eventually led to the "conceptual separation of Latin from Romance" and made Latin a foreign language, although this process was not completed until the Renaissance of the twelfth century or even, in a sense, of the sixteenth century.[12]

One need not agree with Wright's damning judgment of the Carolingian reform of education and his apparent aversion toward establishing standards of grammar and orthography. Likewise, his claim that the pre-Carolingian monolingualism could have continued for centuries without developing into the various Romance languages, similar to the way in which English is spoken in the world today, would appear highly speculative.[13] However, Wright's historical research amply confirms his principal argument about the change in pronouncing Latin, which obviously

---

[11] Wright, *Sociophilological Study of Late Latin*, 99.

[12] Ibid., 34; cf. 14–15.

[13] Ibid., 14. A very different evaluation is given by F.J. Thomson, "SS. Cyril and Methodius and a Mythical Western Heresy: Trilinguism: A Contribution to the Study of Patristic and Mediaeval Theories of Sacred Languages", *Analecta Bollandiana* 110 (1992): 93: "Merovingian Latin had ... degenerated into a confused system in which solecism and incongruity were commonplace and it had become necessary to restore correct norms for use throughout the Empire and to instruct the nobility's children in these norms. It is surely no exaggeration to state that the restoration of the *norma rectitudinis* ensured the maintenance of Latin as the language of west European culture until the Renaissance."

had a great impact on the celebration of the Church's liturgy. For instance, he demonstrates that the difficulties of oral communication between the Anglo-Saxon missionary Wynfreth (Boniface, d. 755) and Pope Gregory II (d. 731) stemmed from the fact that the former had learned Latin as a foreign language with an artificial standard of pronunciation based on the written form of words, whereas the latter, a native of Rome, naturally spoke Latin in a "Romance" way. This would explain Wynfreth's unease in speaking to the Pope, whose manner of expression sounded too informal and familiar to him. He preferred to communicate with Gregory II in writing, because in official correspondence they both observed the same linguistic standards and regulations.[14]

It would seem to me that Wright's theory can also shed light on an exchange of letters between Boniface and Pope Zachary (d. 752): the missionary found in Bavaria that children had been baptized "in nomine patria et filia et spiritus sancti" and considered it necessary to readminister the sacrament. This decision, however, met with the disapproval of the Pope, who did not see this necessity.[15] Zachary came from a Greek family in Calabria, then belonging to the Byzantine Empire, but had spent many years in Rome, where he was a deacon before his election to the See of Peter in 741 and can thus be considered as belonging to the monolingual Romance area. As a quasi-native Latin speaker, he was obviously not preoccupied by the grammatically incorrect endings of the sacramental formula and did not see any reason to suspect a deviation from the profession of faith in

[14] See Wright, *Sociophilological Study of Late Latin*, 99–102.

[15] Cf. the letter of Pope Zachary to Boniface, *Ep.* 68, Monumenta Germaniae Historica, Epistulae Selectae I, 141 (dated July 1, 746).

the Blessed Trinity. For Boniface, on the other hand, the departure from standard grammar and pronunciation was so serious that it raised doubts about the validity of the sacrament.

Speech and Silence

Liturgical prayer is a form of public speech, and one may therefore expect it to be said or sung by the officiating clergy in an audible voice, as would seem to have been the universal rule for Christian worship in the first centuries. In the case of the Eucharist, the celebrant bishop or priest recites prayers in the name and on behalf of the whole assembly, and the people usually respond with "Amen", as elicited by the concluding formula of the prayers themselves.

However, by the eighth century it would appear to have been an established custom in the Roman rite of Mass for parts of the rite to be recited by the celebrant in a low voice, most notably the center of the eucharistic liturgy, the Canon. Its more or less silent recitation became the norm until the liturgical reforms after the Second Vatican Council[16] and continues to this day in what Pope Benedict XVI has established as the "Extraordinary Form", or *usus antiquior*, of the Roman rite.[17] This practice is by no means limited to the Western tradition; on the contrary, Eastern

[16] The permission to pray the Canon aloud in Masses celebrated with a congregation, even when not concelebrated, was given in the Sacred Congregation of Rites' Second Instruction for the Right Implementation of the Constitution on the Sacred Liturgy *Tres abhinc annos* (May 4, 1967), *Acta Apostolicae Sedis* 59 (1967): 442–48, no. 10.

[17] See Benedict XVI, Apostolic Letter *Summorum Pontificum* given Motu Proprio (July 7, 2007), *Acta Apostolicae Sedis* 99 (2007): 777–81; (unofficial) English translation: http://www.catholic-ew.org.uk/content/download/5724/39439/file/Apostolic_Letter_Summorum_Pontificum.pdf.

liturgies, such as the Byzantine Anaphora of Saint John Chrysostom, also contain prayers that are to be said *submissa voce* by the celebrant bishop or priest.[18] In this chapter, I intend to trace the origins of the silent recitation of liturgical prayers in the patristic age and to inquire into its motives.

In his studies on the Jerusalem liturgy of the fourth century, Georg Kretschmar took as his starting point the well-known fact that in Cyril of Jerusalem's *Fifth Mystagogical Catechesis*,[19] which comments on the rite of the Eucharist, no mention is made of certain elements of the Anaphora that could reasonably be expected in this period, including the Institution Narrative, the Anamnesis, and the Rite of Fraction. According to Kretschmar, the bishop would explain to his neophytes only those parts of the rite that they had seen and only those prayers that they had heard in the liturgical celebration. This would mean that some parts of the Eucharistic Prayer were recited in silence.[20] For further evidence, Kretschmar points to Theodore of Mopsuestia's *Catechetical Homily* 16, 10–11, and to Narsai's *Homily on the Mysteries*.[21] The reference to Theodore is intriguing, because

[18] See A. Hänggi and I. Pahl, *Prex eucharistica*, vol. 1: *Textus e variis liturgiis antiquioribus selecti*, 3rd ed., Spicilegium Friburgense 12 (Fribourg: Universitätsverlag, 1998), 223–29.

[19] Recent scholarship has provided convincing arguments for settling the question of the authenticity of the *Mystagogical Catecheses* attributed to Cyril. They may have been preached as late as the 380s, and the lapse of time accounts for the differences between them and the pre-baptismal catecheses from the middle of the fourth century. See, for instance, E. Yarnold, *Cyril of Jerusalem*, The Early Church Fathers (London and New York: Routledge, 2000).

[20] G. Kretschmar, *Studien zur frühchristlichen Trinitätstheologie*, Beiträge zur historischen Theologie 21 (Tübingen: J. C. B. Mohr, 1956), 167.

[21] G. Kretschmar, "Die frühe Geschichte der Jerusalemer Liturgie", *Jahrbuch für Liturgik und Hymnologie* 2 (1956–1957): 28–32. The reference to Theodore is in n. 47 on p. 32.

it could shed light on liturgical practice in Antioch only a decade or so after Cyril's Jerusalem catechesis; however, it is also very unspecific. The passage in question states simply that the congregation joins in the singing of the *Sanctus* and then falls into silence again, while "the priest resumes his holy service", starting the Post-Sanctus with the words "Holy is the Father, holy is the Son, holy is also the Holy Spirit."[22] At this point there is no suggestion that the priest recites this part of the prayer in a low voice.

In a recent contribution, Anthony Gelston notes another passage in Theodore that might sustain Kretschmar's hypothesis. Toward the end of *Catechesis* 16, just before the Rite of Fraction, there is an ambiguity in the text, which Alphonse Mingana translates as "The priest recites quietly these prayers", whereas Raymond Tonneau and Robert Devreesse opt for "Sur ces prières s'arrête le pontife" (With these prayers the priest ends).[23] This means that the priest has completed saying the Eucharistic Prayer and proceeds to the Rite of Fraction. Gelston argues that the Syriac verb (*šl'*) would support either translation, but the context makes that of Tonneau and Devreesse more likely; therefore Kretschmar's argument is precarious.[24] The earliest clear evidence for a

---

[22] Theodore of Mopsuestia, *Hom. cat.* 16, 10, ed. R. Tonneau and R. Devreesse, Studi e Testi 145 (Vatican City: Biblioteca Apostolica Vaticana, 1949), 548.

[23] Theodore of Mopsuestia, *Hom. cat.* 16, 15, ed. A. Mingana, *Commentary of Theodore of Mopsuestia on the Lord's Prayer and on the Sacraments of Baptism and the Eucharist*, Woodbrooke Studies 6 (Cambridge: W. Heffer, 1933), 105, and ed. Tonneau and Devreesse, 557 (fol. 139v).

[24] A. Gelston, "The Meaning of *šl'* in Theodore of Mopsuestia's Sixteenth Catechetical Lecture and the Silent Recitation of the Eucharistic Prayer", *Journal of Theological Studies*, n.s., 60 (2009): 192: "Theodore is saying that it is immediately after the priest has brought the eucharistic prayer to an end that he takes the bread to perform the fraction, rather than that he has recited part of the prayer in silence."

partial recitation of the Eucharistic Prayer in silence is found in Narsai's *Homily on the Mysteries.*[25]

The extant works of Narsai, the head of the theological schools of Edessa and of Nisibis who died at the age of more than a hundred in 502,[26] include the homily usually entitled *On the Mysteries*, one of the most interesting patristic sources on the liturgy.[27] Soon after the publication of this text by Alphonse Mingana in 1905, its authenticity was questioned on two grounds: first, it was doubted whether the ritual solemnity that is described in this homily could reflect the East Syrian liturgy in the late fifth century; secondly, some manuscripts would rather point to an author in the thirteenth century. The latter objection has been refuted, since the homily clearly shows the catechumenate as a living institution, which was no longer the case in the Church of the East in the thirteenth century. As for the first objection, the "highly developed ritualism"[28] of the homily is in continuity with Theodore of Mopsuestia's account of the liturgy of his day in his catechetical homilies, which in fact had a strong influence on the subsequent growth of the East Syrian rite. Sebastian Brock argues on linguistic grounds that the homily dates from a generation

[25] Gelston, "Meaning of *šlʿ*", 192; likewise, G. G. Willis, "The Variable Prayers of the Roman Mass", in *Further Essays in Early Roman Liturgy*, Alcuin Club Collection 50 (London: SPCK, 1968), 126.

[26] Cf. P. Bruns, "Narses von Edessa", in *Lexikon der antiken christlichen Literatur*, ed. S. Döpp and W. Geerlings, 3rd rev. and enlarged ed. (Freiburg: Herder, 2002), 514–15.

[27] Edited by A. Mingana, *Narsai doctoris syri homiliae et carmina* (Mosul: Typis Fratrum Praedicatorum, 1905), 1:270–98; English translation by R. H. Connolly, *The Liturgical Homilies of Narsai*, Texts and Studies 8, 1 (Cambridge: Cambridge University Press, 1909), 1–32.

[28] E. Bishop, "Observations on the Liturgy of Narsai", in Connolly, *Liturgical Homilies of Narsai*, 88.

or two after Narsai, most likely the sixth century.[29] At any rate, it cannot be much later than Narsai's time, and a comparison with direct liturgical sources shows it "to be a reliable witness to East Syrian usage", as E. C. Ratcliff notes.[30]

On the Mysteries suggests that large parts of the Anaphora were prayed by the celebrant in a low voice. After the deacon has read the diptychs and while he is exhorting the people to pray, the priest says a silent prayer, which is followed by the initial dialogue of the part corresponding to the Preface of the Latin tradition.[31] The "Preface" itself, however, is apparently said inaudibly and is described by Narsai thus: "All the ecclesiastical body now observes silence, and all set themselves to pray earnestly in their hearts. The priests are still and the deacons stand in silence, the whole people is quiet and still, subdued and calm. . . . The bright[-robed] priest, the tongue of the Church, opens his mouth and speaks in secret with God as a familiar."[32] The concluding words of this prayer are recited aloud and serve to introduce the singing of the *Sanctus*. Narsai comments: "With these words all the Church cries out and returns to silence. The priest begins to commune with God."[33] It would appear from the homily that the long Post-Sanctus prayer, which is purported to reflect the content of Jesus' own

[29] S. Brock, "Diachronic Aspects of Syriac Word Formation: An Aid for Dating Anonymous Texts", in *V. Symposium Syriacum: Katholieke Universiteit, Leuven, 29–31 août 1988*, ed. R. Lavenant, Orientalia Christiana Analecta 236 (Rome: Pont. Inst. Studiorum Orientalium, 1990), 321–30.

[30] E. C. Ratcliff, "A Note on the Anaphoras Described in the Liturgical Homilies of Narsai", in *Liturgical Studies*, ed. A. H. Couratin and D. H. Tripp (London: SPCK, 1976), 67.

[31] Narsai, *Hom.* XVII (*De mysteriis*), in Connolly, *Liturgical Homilies of Narsai*, 11.

[32] Ibid., 12.

[33] Ibid., 13.

thanksgiving at the Last Supper,[34] is recited quietly in its entirety; it concludes with an *ecphonesis*[35] and the people's response. Narsai observes: "To this effect the priest gives thanks before God, and he raises his voice at the end of his prayer to make it audible to the people. He makes his voice heard, and with his hand he signs the Mysteries that are set [on the altar]; and the people with *Amen* concur and acquiesce in the prayer of the priest."[36]

The liturgical practice emerging from Narsai's homily is confirmed by subsequent witnesses to the East Syrian tradition that are only a little later than Narsai: a short description of the liturgy by Catholicos Iso'yahb I (581/582 to 595/596),[37] which is included in the *Synodicon Orientale* and the more detailed liturgical commentary of Gabriel of Qatar (written between 615 and 625).[38]

---

[34] The author attributes his Anaphora directly to Theodore—W. F. Macomber, "An Anaphora Prayer Composed by Theodore of Mopsuestia", *Parole de l'Orient* 6–7 (1975–1976), 341–47, considers this ascription correct—and claims Nestorius as the model for his summary of the intercessions. See Narsai, *Hom.* XVII (*De mysteriis*), in Connolly, *Liturgical Homilies of Narsai*, 20.

[35] An *ecphonesis* is a liturgical exclamation chanted aloud by a priest or deacon as part of a litany or at the end of a prayer; it is distinguished from the portions that are to be said silently.

[36] Narsai, *Hom.* XVII (*De mysteriis*), in Connolly, *Liturgical Homilies of Narsai*, 18.

[37] See his *Letter to James, Bishop of Darai*, in *Synodicon Orientale ou Recueil de synodes nestoriens*, ed. J.B. Chabot (Paris: Imprimerie Nationale, 1902), 168–69 [428]; cf. S.Y.H. Jammo, *La structure de la messe chaldéenne du début jusqu'à l'anaphore*, Orientalia Christiana Analecta 207 (Rome: Pontificium Institutum Orientalium Studiorum, 1979), 21.

[38] Gabriel of Qatar, *Memra* V, 2, 66–67 (British Library, Or. 3336, fol. 201v–202r), published in the Syriac original and in an English translation by S.P. Brock, "Gabriel of Qatar's Commentary on the Liturgy", *Hugoye: Journal of Syriac Studies* 6/2 (2003): http://syrcom.cua.edu/Hugoye/Vol6No2/HV6N2Brock.html (accessed August 29, 2011). See also S.Y.H. Jammo, "Gabriel Qatraya et son commentaire sur la liturgie chaldéenne", *Orientalia Christiana Periodica* 32 (1966): 39–52.

The custom of reciting large parts of the Anaphora in silence also spread to Greek-speaking churches by the middle of the sixth century, as we can infer from Emperor Justinian's legislation against it. The *Novella* of March 26, 565, stipulated that the prayers of the eucharistic and baptismal liturgies must be said by the celebrant bishop or priest in "a voice that can be heard by the faithful people", so that their minds may be elevated to greater compunction and to the praise of God.[39]

In support of this legislation, the emperor cites 1 Corinthians 14:16–17, a text already used by Ambrosiaster in his comments on liturgy and language: "Otherwise, if you bless with the spirit, how can any one in the position of an outsider say the 'Amen' to your thanksgiving when he does not know what you are saying. For you may give thanks well enough, but the other man is not edified", and also Romans 10:10: "For man believes with his heart and so is justified, and he confesses with his lips and so is saved."

The context of the specific injunction that "the prayers made in the Holy Oblation and elsewhere should be said in an audible voice" is a longer piece of ecclesiastical legislation, in which Justinian states his intention to enforce clerical discipline: "We have received various complaints as to such non-observance by clerics and monks and some bishops as not conducting themselves in accordance with the holy canons; and others have been found who do not know even the prayer of the Holy Oblation or of Holy Baptism."[40]

It is highly unlikely that an ecclesiastical legislator would rule against a practice that had not yet manifested itself. For

---

[39] Justinian, *Nouellae*, 137, 6, in *Corpus Iuris Ciuilis*, vol. 3: *Nouellae*, ed. R. Schoell and G. Kroll, 6th ed. (Berlin: Weidmann, 1954), 699.

[40] Ibid., in the translation of Bishop, "Observations on the Liturgy of Narsai", 123.

this reason, it is safe to conclude that the custom to recite liturgical prayers silently must have extended to some degree into the last year of Justinian's reign. The fact that the extant Latin version of this particular legislation is not contained in the official sixth-century Latin text of the *Novellae* known as the *Authenticum* suggests that it was originally published only in Greek.[41] It would appear, therefore, that the practice in question arose at first in the Greek-speaking parts of the empire.

There is a remarkable anecdote in John Moschus' *Pratum spirituale*, written in the last quarter of the sixth century: three boys in Palestine, while tending their sheep, decided to play and reenact the eucharistic liturgy. They set up everything as best as they could, and one of them, taking the role of the priest, repeated the words of the Anaphora, which he knew by heart. When they arrived at the Rite of Fraction, fire came from heaven, destroyed their "altar", and nearly killed them. Recovering, they told the local bishop what had happened, and he built a monastery in the place where the miraculous event happened. The most relevant aspect of this story for our argument is the reason given for why the boys were so familiar with the words of the Anaphora. They regularly attended church: "And since in some places the priests are accustomed to pray aloud, the children

[41] This is noted by Bishop, "Observations on the Liturgy of Narsai", 122, n. 1. Perhaps it should also be taken into account that the *Novella* dates from the last few months of Justinian's reign, when his ecclesiastical policy became more and more erratic, as exemplified in his endorsement of "aphthartodocetic" Christology; cf. A. Grillmeier, *Christ in Christian Tradition*, vol. 2, pt. 2: *The Church of Constantinople in the Sixth Century*, ed. T. Hainthaler, trans. J. Cawte and P. Allen (London: Mowbray; Louisville, Ky.: Westminster John Knox Press, 1995), 468–73, and the severe judgment of E. Schwartz, *Zur Kirchenpolitik Justinians*, Sitzungsberichte der Bayerischen Akademie der Wissenschaften zu München, Philosophisch-Historische Abteilung, 1940/2 (Munich: Beck, 1940), 277, where he speaks of the emperor's "senile decay".

found that they had learned the prayer of the holy oblation, because they had often heard it being said."[42] The way John Moschus presents this would imply that in his day it was more common in Palestine not to recite the Anaphora in an audible voice.

By the time of Justinian's *Novella* of 565, the practice of reciting the Canon quietly had not yet made its way to Rome. This is reflected in various sources containing material dating from around that time.[43] Thus the Old Gelasian Sacramentary notes for the Mass of the Scrutinies on the Third Sunday of Lent, which is believed to belong to the earlier stratum of the Gelasian tradition,[44] that the celebrant pauses in the *Memento Domine* prayer of the Canon while the names of the sponsors are read out; likewise he pauses in the *Hanc igitur* while the names of the candidates for baptism are read out, possibly in both instances by a deacon.[45] This custom echoes the practice current in the pontificate of Pope Innocent I of announcing within the prayer the names of those who had brought offerings.[46]

---

[42] John Moschus, *Pratum spirituale*, 196: PG 87:3081; cf. 3080–84.

[43] Cf. G. G. Willis, *A History of Early Roman Liturgy to the Death of Pope Gregory the Great*, Henry Bradshaw Society, Subsidia 1 (London: Boydell Press, 1994), 36–38.

[44] See E. C. Ratcliff and A. H. Couratin, "The Roman *Canon Missae*: Its Beginnings and Early Background", in *Liturgical Studies*, 101.

[45] *Sacramentum Gelasianum*, 195 and 197, in *Liber Sacramentorum Romanae Aeclesiae Ordinis Anni Circuli*, ed. L. C. Mohlberg, Rerum Ecclesiasticarum Documenta: Series maior, Fontes IV, 3rd ed. (Rome: Herder, 1981), 33; cf. *Ordo Romanus* [= *OR*] XI, 34–35, in *Les Ordines Romani du haut moyen âge*, ed. M. Andrieu, 5 vols., Spicilegium Sacrum Lovaniense 11, 23, 24, 28, 29 (Louvain: Peeters, 1931–1961), 2:425–26.

[46] Innocent I, *Letter to Decentius*, 2, in *La lettre du pape Innocent I à Decentius de Gubbio (19 mars 416): Texte critique, traduction e commentaire*, ed. R. Cabié, Bibliothèque de la Revue d'histoire ecclésiastique 58 (Louvain: Publications Universitaires, 1973), 22.

Between the latter part of the sixth century and the second half of the eighth century, liturgical practice in Rome developed in such a way that by the year 800, the Canon of the Mass was recited by the celebrant in a low voice. This development cannot be traced before the appearance of the *Ordines Romani* in the middle of the eighth century, although these important sources for the papal liturgy may well reflect a practice that had been established for some time. *Ordo Romanus* I, which describes the Papal Mass in Rome around 750, notes that, after the singing of the *Sanctus*, "surgit pontifex solus et intrat in canonem".[47] There are scholars who take this passage as an indication that the Canon was said in silence, but in fact this is not entirely clear. What it says is that the pope alone, having bowed with his assistants during the *Sanctus*, stands upright and "enters into the Canon", that is, he alone continues with the prayer *Te igitur*,[48] while the clergy assisting him remain bowing. The passage does not specify whether or not he prays in an audible voice. However, what is significant is that here, unlike in the earlier tradition, a clear distinction is introduced between the Preface, which is sung aloud and culminates in the *Sanctus* chanted by the schola, and the "Canon" beginning with the words *Te igitur*.[49] This distinction is reflected in liturgical manuscripts

[47] *OR* I, 88: Andrieu, *Ordines Romani*, 2:95–96.

[48] J. A. Jungmann, *Missarum Sollemnia: Eine genetische Erklärung der römischen Messe*, 2 vols., 5th ed. (Vienna: Herder, 1962), 130, n. 15, observes that the verb *intrare* is used precisely in this sense in the *Gelasianum*, 195, 319, and 381.

[49] However, the same *Ordo Romanus* I still reflects the older understanding of the Canon beginning with the "Preface", when it indicates: "Nam quod intermisimus de patena, quando inchoat canonem, venit acolytes sub humero habens sindonem in collo ligatam, tenens patenam ante pectus suum in parte dextera usque medium canonem"; *OR* I, 91: Andrieu, *Ordines Romani*, 2:96–97.

from the ninth century onward, where the title *Canon Missae* or *Canon actionis* is often inserted before *Te igitur*.

As could be expected, the development toward a completely silent Canon was a gradual one. *Ordo Romanus* III, 1, an addition to the first *Ordo Romanus* dating from the late eighth century, specifies the concelebration of cardinal priests with the pope on the four most solemn occasions of the liturgical year: Easter, Pentecost, Saint Peter (and Saint Paul), and Christmas. The cardinal priests standing around the altar are to say the Canon in a lower voice than the pope: "ut vox pontificis valentius audiatur".[50] This would obviously imply that the Canon is said in an audible voice.

Further light on this may be shed by *Ordo Romanus* XV, also known under its title *Capitulare ecclesiastici ordinis*, which is an early Frankish recension of the first *Ordo Romanus* from about the middle of the eighth century. Interestingly, this *Ordo* distinguishes between various ways of reciting the different parts of the Eucharistic Prayer. The Preface is sung in an elevated voice so that it may be heard by all;[51] after the singing of the *Sanctus*, the pontiff begins to recite the Canon in a different voice so that it may be heard only by those standing around the altar.[52] He raises his voice again only at the end, for the *ecphonesis* "Per omnia saecula saeculorum".[53]

---

[50] *OR* III, 1: Andrieu, *Ordines Romani*, 2:131.

[51] *OR* XV, 37: Andrieu, *Ordines Romani*, 3:103: "Inde vero pontifex, elevans vocem et dicit ipsa prefationem, ita ut ab omnibus audiatur."

[52] *OR* XV, 39: Andrieu, *Ordines Romani*, 3:103: "Et incipit canire [varia lectio: pontifex canone] dissimili voce ⟨et melodia⟩, ut a circumstantibus altare tantum audiatur." The variant readings at this point need not concern us. Whether or not the Canon was chanted in a reciting tone, it would still be audible only to bystanders.

[53] *OR* XV, 43: Andrieu, *Ordines Romani*, 3:104: ". . . usquedum dixerit pontifex alta voce: Per omnia saecula saeculorum."

Ordo Romanus V, a redaction of the first *Ordo Romanus* dating from the late ninth century, notes that after the singing of the *Sanctus*: "surgit solus pontifex et tacito intrat in canonem",[54] adding the specification "tacito" or "silently" to the original rubric. This might not necessarily mean that the Canon was completely inaudible, but at any rate it would be heard only by those who were close to the altar.

What may have been the motives for the development that has been sketched in this chapter? The recitation of liturgical prayers *submissa voce* is often attributed to the increasing sense of reverence and awe toward the mysteries celebrated in the liturgy, which is tangible especially in the Eastern Christian traditions from the fourth century onward. Two decisive factors are believed to be decisive: the emphasis on the divinity of Christ in opposition to Arianism and the concern to protect the sacred from the uncatechized masses that were flocking into churches after the Constantinian settlement.[55]

The *Ordines Romani* of the eighth century present the Canon of the Mass, now understood to begin with *Te igitur*, as a "holy of holies", into which only the pontiff could enter. This idea would eventually lead to an entirely silent recitation of the Canon, at least from the perspective of the lay faithful. It is of course conceivable that this practice was introduced in Rome by the popes of Greek and Syrian origin who were elected to the See of Peter in the second half of the seventh century and the first half of the eighth century. I should like to suggest that in the case of the Roman liturgy, there may be other considerations, above all, the

---

[54] *OR* V, 58: Andrieu, *Ordines Romani*, 2:221.

[55] See, for instance, Kretschmar, *Studien zur frühchristlichen Trinitätstheologie*, 167.

architectural setting of the solemn celebrations of the Roman pontiff. When the pope celebrated Mass in one of the large Roman basilicas, such as the Lateran, Saint Peter's in the Vatican, or Saint Paul's Outside the Walls, before the existence of electrical amplification, it would have been impossible in most parts of the church to follow the prayers he recited or chanted at the altar. Even in a smaller church like Saint Sabina, the audibility of the liturgical prayers would have been much limited. Just as there were visible obstructions, such as the relatively high *cancelli* separating the various precincts of the church's interior[56] and a ciborium over the main altar, sometimes decorated with curtains, so the physical dimensions of the church interior created an acoustic obstruction between the pope and his assistants at the altar and the faithful in the naves.[57]

The *Ordines Romani* describing liturgical practice in the city of Rome would not need to specify this, but when they were adapted to Frankish conditions, and thus to churches of medium or small size, it was actually written down that the Canon was to be recited in a low voice. This interpretation would, in my view, account for the development observed from *Ordo Romanus* I to *Ordo Romanus* V. Thus the emergence of the silent Canon in the Western tradition should also be seen in the context of the liturgy's architectural setting, which had an impact on the relation between speech and silence.

Finally, the historical development in the West that I have traced, motivated as it was in part by architectural considerations, was further shaped and fostered by theological

---

[56] This is still visibile in the Roman Basilica of Saint Clement, which contains *cancelli* dating from late antiquity.

[57] Cf. Willis, "Variable Prayers of the Roman Mass", 128–29.

reflection on the nature of the eucharistic sacrifice and its cult. It has already been observed how Eastern authors such as Narsai defended the practice of the *submissa vox* theologically as a sign of the priest's "familiarity" with God or of his "communing" with him. A similar dynamic, in which speculative theology dialectically engages and solidifies liturgical practice, was to emerge in the Latin West as well. In the next chapter, we turn to one of the clearest and most brilliant representatives of this tradition.

V

SAINT THOMAS AQUINAS ON LITURGY AND LANGUAGE

This chapter will explore Saint Thomas Aquinas' reflections on the language of the liturgy. At first sight, it seems that he has little to say on this subject. This would not be surprising, because the thirteenth-century scholastic was far removed from the formative period of liturgical Latin in late antiquity, which has been studied in the previous chapters of this book. Aquinas and his contemporaries would have simply taken it for granted that Latin was the language of worship in Western Christendom. This is not to suggest that there was no growth of the liturgy in the High Middle Ages; on the contrary, there were significant additions to the Church's liturgical year, such as the feast of Corpus Christi, for which Aquinas composed the office. Moreover, there was an ongoing development of rites and ceremonies, which went along with momentous achievements in sacred music, art, and architecture. However, the principal parts of the eucharistic liturgy, above all the Canon of the Mass, the Prefaces, and the prayers for the temporal cycle had been fixed centuries before. This *lex orandi*, expressing the *lex credendi* of the Roman Church, provided for Aquinas a stable point of reference in his theological argument, as an even cursory look on the *Summa* shows, where he frequently refers to the *consuetudo Ecclesiae* as an authority.

The Mass as a Representation of Christ's Passion

For the purpose of this inquiry, it will be useful to give a brief account of Aquinas' understanding of the eucharistic liturgy as a representation of Christ's Passion, which is found in his exposition of the rite of Mass in question 83 of the *Tertia Pars* of the *Summa*.[1] The first article of this question, which is entitled "Whether Christ is sacrificed in this sacrament", provides the groundwork for the subsequent articles. As the title indicates, Aquinas discusses the sacrificial character of the Eucharist in a sacramental and liturgical context. In the celebration of the sacrament, we are drawn into the presence of the one sacrifice Christ offered on the Cross. After quoting Saint Augustine in the *sed contra* ("Christ was sacrificed once in himself and yet he is sacrificed daily in the sacrament"),[2] Thomas explains the sacrificial character of the Mass in the body of the article:

> The celebration of this sacrament is called a sacrifice for two reasons. First, because, as Augustine says (*Ad Simplician. ii*), "the images of things are called by the names of

[1] The following discussion is greatly indebted to M. Levering, *Sacrifice and Community: Jewish Offering and Christian Eucharist* (Oxford: Blackwell, 2005), 82–93.

[2] III, q. 83, a. 1, *sed contra*. The quotation from Augustine is *Ep. 98*: PL 33:363–64. The works of Aquinas are cited according to the editions made available on http://www.corpusthomisticum.org, unless otherwise noted. Translations of the *Summa* follow the rendering of the Fathers of the English Dominican Province, *The Summa theologica*, 22 vols., 2nd rev. ed. (London: Burns, Oates & Washbourne, 1912–1936).

> the things whereof they are the images; as when we look upon a picture or a fresco, we say, 'This is Cicero and that is Sallust'." But, as was said above (q. 79, a. 1), the celebration of this sacrament is an image representing Christ's Passion, which is His true sacrifice. Accordingly the celebration of this sacrament is called Christ's sacrifice. Hence it is that Ambrose, in commenting on Hebrews 10:1, says: "In Christ was offered up a sacrifice capable of giving eternal salvation; what then do we do? Do we not offer it up every day in memory of His death?" [3]

Here we find Aquinas' key idea that the sacrament of the Eucharist is an *imago repraesentativa* of Christ's Passion. Following Anscar Vonier's classic study of the subject,[4] Thierry-Dominique Humbrecht comments on the importance of sacramental "representation" in Aquinas, a concept that can be traced back to Augustine and was used by Hugh of Saint Victor and Peter Lombard.[5] Humbrecht also shows that the Angelic Doctor's use of this idea is very supple. Here the presence of Christ's sacrifice in the Mass is understood in a very concrete, literal fashion: the altar represents the Cross on which the Lord gave his life for our salvation, and the priest, who through receiving the sacrament of Holy Orders has been conformed to Christ the High Priest, acts and speaks as the image representing Christ the Head.[6]

---

[3] III, q. 83, a. 1, *resp.*

[4] A. Vonier, *A Key to the Doctrine of the Eucharist* (London: Burns, Oates & Washbourne, 1925).

[5] T.-D. Humbrecht, "L'Eucharistie, 'représentation' du sacrifice du Christ, selon saint Thomas", *Revue Thomiste* 98 (1998): 363.

[6] III, q. 83, a. 1 ad 2 and 3. Cf. P. M. Candler, "Liturgically Trained Memory: A Reading of *Summa Theologiae* III.83", *Modern Theology* 19 (2004): 423–55. In a certain sense, Christ's sacrifice was present even in the sacraments of the Old Law, Aquinas adds, quoting from Revelation 13:8: "Whose names are not written in the Book of Life of the Lamb, which was slain from the

The second reason for understanding the Mass as a sacrifice, according to Aquinas, is with respect to the effect of his Passion (*quantum ad effectum passionis*):

> . . . because by this sacrament, we are made partakers of the fruit of our Lord's Passion. Hence in one of the Sunday Secrets we say: "Whenever the commemoration of this sacrifice is celebrated, the work of our redemption is accomplished."[7]

The two aspects of the Eucharist as the visible, albeit figurative, representation of Christ's Passion and the invisible efficacy of this sacrifice are consistently combined in Aquinas' explanation of the rite. Notably, the sacrament is also a representation of Christ's Resurrection; in the liturgy of the Mass, the priest turns toward the people five times with the greeting "The Lord be with you", Aquinas explains, "to denote that our Lord manifested Himself five times on the day of his Resurrection"; a bishop, he adds, "when he celebrates on festival days, in his first greeting says, 'Peace be to you', which was our Lord's greeting after the Resurrection, whose person the bishop chiefly represents".[8] Hence, Aquinas' idea of sacramental representation, while being focused on the Cross, encompasses the whole of the Paschal Mystery. Accordingly, Thomas prefaces his brief exposition of the rite of Mass in the body of article 4 by emphasizing that: "The whole mystery of our salvation is comprised in

---

beginning of the world". Cf. also *Super Sent.*, lib. 4, d. 8, q. 2, a. 4, qc. 3 expos.: "Sacramenta autem quae in lege naturae fiebant, non erant figurae sacramentorum veteris legis, sed magis passionis Christi."

[7] III, q. 83, a. 1, *resp*. The quote ("quoties huius hostiae commemoratio celebratur, opus nostrae redemptionis exercetur") is from the Secret of the Ninth Sunday after Pentecost in the Extraordinary Form of the Roman Rite, now also the Prayer over the Offerings for the Second Sunday of the Year and for the Mass of the Last Supper on Maundy Thursday in the Ordinary Form.

[8] III, q. 83, a. 5 ad 6. See also ad 8.

this sacrament" (In hoc sacramento totum mysterium nostrae salutis comprehenditur).[9]

Aquinas' exposition of the prayers and rites of Mass is indebted to the allegorical method of liturgical commentary, which has its roots in patristic authors, such as Cyril of Jerusalem, Ambrose of Milan, Theodore of Mopsuestia, and Pseudo-Dionysius the Areopagite, and was shaped decisively in the Western tradition by Amalarius' *De officio missae* in the third book of *De ecclesiasticis officiis*, written between 827 and 832.[10] Amalarius favors the spiritual sense of the liturgy over the letter of the prayers and ceremonies, in the threefold distinction familiar from scriptural exegesis: the allegorical sense, by which the Old Testament announces and foreshadows the New; the tropological or moral sense; and the anagogical sense, relating to the things that are above.

Amalarius has a strong preference for an allegorical interpretation of the liturgy in a "rememorative" manner: he consistently interprets the rites and ceremonies of the Mass as reenacting the saving acts of Christ.[11] Every word and gesture of the priest and his assistants is charged with symbolic

---

[9] III, q. 83, a. 4, *resp*. Cf. B.D. Marshall, "The Whole Mystery of Our Salvation: Saint Thomas Aquinas on the Eucharist as Sacrifice", in *Rediscovering Aquinas and the Sacraments: Studies in Sacramental Theology*, ed. M. Levering and M. Dauphinais (Chicago: Hillenbrand, 2009), 39–64.

[10] For a contemporary explanation of liturgical allegoresis, see M.P. Foley, "The Mystic Meaning of the *Missale Romanum*", *Antiphon* 13 (2009): 103–25.

[11] The method of rememorative allegory has been severely criticized by twentieth-century liturgists; more recently, however, it has been viewed more favorably: F. Quoëx, "Thomas d'Aquin, mystagogue: *L'Expositio Missae de la Somme de théologie* (IIIa, q. 83, a. 4–5)", *Revue Thomiste* 105 (2005): 179–225 and 435–472; C. Barthe, "The 'Mystical' Meaning of the Ceremonies of the Mass: Liturgical Exegesis in the Middle Ages", in *The Genius of the Roman Liturgy: Historical Diversity and Spiritual Reach: Proceedings of the 2006 Oxford CIEL Colloquium*, ed. U.M. Lang (Chicago: Hillenbrand, 2010), 179–97.

meaning because it manifests the presence of Christ and his work of redemption in the solemn worship of the Church. Although soon after the publication of Amalarius' work there was a reaction against rememorative-allegorical interpretation of the liturgy, exemplified by the Deacon Florus of Lyon, who wrote his *Opusculum de actione missarum* between 835 and 838, this method was generally received among later authors. Thomas' master, Albert the Great, was somewhat critical of it, but the most widely read liturgical commentators of the age of the cathedrals were disciples of Amalarius, among them John Beleth (d. 1182) in his *Summa de ecclesiasticis officiis*; Prevostinus of Cremona (d. 1210) in his *Summa de officiis*; Sicard of Cremona (d. ca. 1215) in his voluminous *Mitrale seu de officiis ecclesiasticis summa*; Lothar of Segni (later Pope Innocent III, d. 1216) in his *De sacro altaris mysterio*; and, above all, William Durandus (d. 1296) in his *Rationale divinorum officiorum*, the most complete and most influential liturgical *summa* of the Middle Ages.

Consistent with his biblical hermeneutics as outlined in the opening question of the *Summa*,[12] Aquinas does not so much choose between a literal and allegorical reading of the prayers and rites of the Mass as embrace both in balance.[13] A striking example of this is found in article 5 of question 83, "Whether the actions performed in celebrating this sacrament are fitting". Against the objection that several of the celebrant priest's ritual gestures at Mass are "ridiculous", such as making the sign of the cross many times over the eucharistic species, even after the Consecration, stretching out the arms after the Consecration as Christ

[12] I, q. 1, aa. 9–10.

[13] For more on this point, see Foley, "The Mystic Meaning", 109–10 and 120.

did on the Cross, Aquinas first refers to the "practice of the Church, which cannot err, since she is taught by the Holy Spirit".[14] Secondly, he defends them on the grounds that "they are done so as to represent something else." The priest's extending his arms after the Consecration was a common liturgical gesture in a number of medieval liturgies and was kept in the Dominican rite, even after it ceased to be observed in the Roman rite.[15] Aquinas takes it to signify "the outstretching of Christ's arms upon the cross".[16] Peter Candler's comments are to the point:

> Thus the function of this gesture is to remind the communicant of Christ's sacrifice.... The gesture is important because it not only teaches us about Christ's death as an offering for us, but it also aims at persuading us to participate in that sacrifice.... By imaging this body, the priest re-performs the divine initiative of making the church one body through Christ's sacrifice. The reference to the body of Christ on the cross requires the trope, learned in liturgical practice, that these outstretched arms point not to themselves but to another body, which we are to become.[17]

[14] "Ecclesiae consuetudo, quae errare non potest, utpote spiritu sancto instructa": III, q. 83, a. 5, *sed contra.*

[15] When Aquinas comments on the Mass, he does so "secundum consuetudinem romanae Ecclesiae" (III, q. 64, a. 2 ad 1), that is, following the rite of Roman Church, or, more precisely, the rite of the Roman Curia, as revised by Franciscan liturgists. At the initiative of Pope Innocent III and his successors, and owing to the rapid expansion of the Franciscan order, this unified form of the Roman Rite spread fast throughout Europe. It was codified, with remarkable little variation, in the first printed *Missale Romanum* of 1474 and then in the Missal of Pope Pius V, published in 1570. Aquinas consciously chose to base his liturgical commentaries on the rite most widely used in Western Christendom, not on the rite of Mass proper to the Dominicans, which was fixed in 1256 by the Master of the Order of Preachers, Humbert de Romans.

[16] III, q. 83, a. 5 ad 5.

[17] Candler, "Liturgically Trained Memory", 425–26.

Aquinas' liturgical commentary is firmly rooted in his theological synthesis and, more specifically, in his understanding of the Eucharist as a representation of Christ's Passion. It is against this background that I would now like to turn to the long *expositio textus* in the *Scriptum* on the *Sentences*, where Aquinas elaborates on the rite of Mass.[18] At the end of the *expositio*, he notes:

> Let it be known that in the celebration of the Mass, where the Passion is re-presented, certain Greek words are used, such as *kyrie eleison*, which means "Lord, have mercy"; certain Hebrew [words], such as *alleluja*, which means "praise God"; *Sabaoth*, which means "of the hosts"; *hosanna*, which means "save, I pray"; *amen*, which means "truly", or "so be it"; and certain Latin [words], which is obvious; for in these three languages the title of Christ's Cross was written (Jn 19).[19]

The first thing to note here is Aquinas' debt to the patristic tradition of the *tres linguae sacrae*, which has been briefly discussed in chapter 2 (see above, pp. 48–50). In particular, the Angelic Doctor takes up and develops Augustine's exegesis in his own commentary on the Gospel of John: Hebrew, Greek, and Latin excel among all other languages because of the providential role they had in the history of salvation.[20]

---

[18] The discussion here differs from the one in the *Summa Theologiae* at various points, but I cannot dwell on these here; see P.-M. Gy, "Avancées du traité de l'eucharistie de S. Thomas dans la *somme* par rapport aux *Sentences*", *Revue des sciences philosophiques et théologiques* 77 (1993): 219–28.

[19] "Sciendum autem, quod in officio Missae, ubi passio repraesentatur, quaedam continentur verba Graeca, sicut, *kyrie eleison*, idest domine miserere: quaedam Hebraica, sicut *alleluja*, idest laudate Deum; *Sabaoth*, idest exercituum; *hosanna*, salva obsecro; *amen*, idest vere, vel fiat: quaedam Latina, quae patent: quia his tribus linguis scriptus est titulus crucis Christi, *Joan*. 19." *Super Sent*., lib. 4, d. 8, q. 2, a. 4, qc. 3 expos.

[20] See Thomas Aquinas, *Super Io*., c. 19, l. 4.

It would seem that the oldest comment on the use of these three languages in the liturgy is found in the so-called *Brief Exposition of the Gallican Liturgy*, once attributed to Germanus of Paris (ca. 496–576) but now dated to the seventh or early eighth century. This text provides a summary account of the rite of Mass and observes that the *Trishagion*, which came before the Canticle of Zechariah (*Benedictus*) and the Scripture reading in the Gallican liturgy, is sung first in Greek, then in Latin, and finishes with the Hebrew *amen*, thus symbolizing the *trinitas linguarum* of the title of the Cross.[21] This is a mere description of fact, and no normative conclusions are drawn from it.

Going back to Aquinas' *expositio* from the *Scriptum* on the *Sentences*, the most important theological point in my opinion is hidden in a subordinate clause, when he speaks about the *officium Missae*, "where the Passion is re-presented" (ubi passio repraesentatur). With this comment, Aquinas goes beyond the historical rationale for the use of Hebrew, Greek, and Latin in Christian worship; he also provides a theological argument for it: because the Mass is a representation of the Lord's Passion, the languages used in its celebration are those found on the title of the Lord's Cross. It would appear that this idea is not expressed in medieval commentators on the liturgy before Aquinas,[22] with the exception of

[21] The text of Martène's *editio princeps* in PL 72:89C–90A is corrupt; see now the critical edition by P. Bernard, *Epistulae de ordine sacrae oblationis et de diversis charismatibus ecclesiae Germano Parisiensi episcopo adscriptae*: *Epistola I*, 3: CCCM 187:339.

[22] William Durandus (d. 1296), who wrote his *Rationale* more than a decade after the death of Aquinas, is obviously indebted to him: "Notandum est etiam quod in misse officio, ubi passio Christi representatur, tribus linguarum generibus utimur: scilicet greca, hebrea et latina": *Rationale divinorum officiorum* IV, i, 36: CCCM 140:252–53; cf. VI, lxxvii, 14: CCCM 140A:375–76. However, two authors whose influence on Durandus is evident in many

Robert Paululus of Amiens (d. after 1180).[23] This lesser-known author is believed to have been associated with Hugh of Saint Victor, who, as mentioned above, develops the concept of representation in his treatise on the sacraments. The use of this concept as a hermeneutical key to understanding the rite is thus not original to Aquinas, but it is his achievement to integrate the idea into the architecture of his *Summa* and so to provide it with theological depth. From a modern perspective, the argument may be considered unsatisfactory, but for Aquinas, the use of the three languages is part of the sacramental representation constitutive of the sacred liturgy.

Mystery of Faith

In question 83 of the *Tertia Pars* of the *Summa*, Aquinas observes on the "instruction of the faithful people" (instructio fidelis populi), that is, the "Mass of the Catechumens" or "Liturgy of the Word": "There precedes, in the second place, the instruction of the faithful, because this sacrament is 'a mystery of faith', as stated above."[24] The expression *mysterium fidei* is explained earlier, in the context of the formula of consecration of the chalice. "Mystery" is used here of a reality that is contained in the sacrament in a hidden

places do not formulate this theological idea: John Beleth, *Summa de divinis officiis*, c. 35 and 98: PL 202:44C and 102BC; Sicard of Cremona, *Mitrale* III, 2: PL 213:96CD.

[23] Robertus Paululus, *De caeremoniis sacramentis, officiis et observationibus ecclesiasticis*, II, 12: PL 177:418A: "Notandum quod tribus linguis, Hebraica, Graeca et Latina missa celebratur, quia his titulus passionis Domini nostri Iesu Christi, cuius repraesentatio missa est, scriptus fuisse legitur. Hebraicum quippe est Alleluia, Hosanna, et Amen. Graecum vero Kyrie eleison; Latinum reliquum officium."

[24] III, q. 83, a. 4, *resp.*

way; not just prefigured or foreshadowed, as in the Old Testament, but present under the veil of the sacramental sign.[25] The link with the formula of consecration of the chalice indicates that "instruction" within the liturgy is always oriented toward the celebration of mystery, which is offered as sacrifice and received as sacrament. Thomas would have been content with the statement of the Second Vatican Council's Constitution on the Sacred Liturgy that "The two parts which, in a certain sense, go to make up the Mass, namely, the liturgy of the word and the eucharistic liturgy, are so closely connected with each other that they form but *one single act of worship*."[26]

At this point Aquinas is more terse than other liturgical commentators of his age, who see in the subdeacon chanting the Epistle a representation of the Old Testament prophets waiting for Christ or, indeed, of John the Baptist pointing toward the one he recognizes as the Lamb of God. Stressing the "dispositive" or preparatory character of this part of the liturgy, Saint Thomas simply describes the lessons from the prophets and apostles read by the lectors and subdeacons, followed by the singing of the Gradual, signifying "progress in life", and of the Alleluia, denoting "spiritual joy", or the Tract on penitential days. Then "the people are instructed perfectly by Christ's teaching contained in the Gospel, which is read by the higher ministers, that is, by the deacons."[27]

It is worth noting that both in the commentary on the *Sentences* and in the *Summa* the standard form of celebration on which he chooses to comment is the Solemn High Mass, where the subdeacon and deacon (and on certain

[25] III, q. 78, a. 3 ad 5.

[26] Second Vatican Council, Constitution on the Sacred Liturgy *Sacrosanctum concilium* (December 4, 1963), no. 56 (italics mine).

[27] III, q. 83, a. 4, *resp.*

occasions, the ordained lector) exercise their specific liturgical roles. The proclamation of the Word of God in the sacred liturgy does not have a simply catechetical function; rather, it has a latreutic character, which is evident when it is carried out in a solemn way with the chanting of the pericope and especially the Gospel procession with candles and incense. The presence of Christ in the Sacred Scriptures gives this part of the Mass a quasi-sacramental quality and so leads the faithful to the offering of the sacrifice of Christ and to receiving Christ in the sacrament. Thus Aquinas concludes his short description by saying: "After the people have been prepared and instructed, the next step is to proceed to the celebration of the mystery."[28]

The kind of instruction that prepares the people to participate in the "Mass of the Faithful" or "Liturgy of the Eucharist" is explicitly distinguished from the kind of instruction that prepares catechumens to receive the sacrament of baptism.[29] Nonetheless, the question arises as to how this *instructio fidelis populi* happened, given the distance between the Latin of the liturgy and the language spoken by the people. Aquinas himself shows a keen awareness of this question in his commentary on 1 Corinthians 14.[30] However,

[28] Ibid.

[29] Ibid., ad 4.

[30] This part of Aquinas' *Expositio et Lectura super Epistolas Pauli Apostoli*, which may originate from his teaching in Rome from 1265 to 1268, is extant only in the form of notes from his course, according to J.-P. Torrell, *Saint Thomas Aquinas*, vol. 1: *The Person and His Work*, trans. R. Royal (Washington, D.C.: Catholic University of America Press, 1996), 250–57 and 340. *The Lectura* on 1 Corinthians 14 is obviously influenced by Ambrosiaster, whose work was transmitted under the authority of Saint Ambrose in the Middle Ages and was cited in the *Glossa Ordinaria* as well as in Peter Lombard's *Sentences*. Aquinas' exposition is not always clear, and, in the absence of a critical edition, it is very difficult to give a coherent interpretation of it. Cf. the discussion of R. Wielockx, "Au sujet du commentaire de saint Thomas sur le 'Corpus

even when the readings were proclaimed in Latin, this did not mean that they were not understood at all by the faithful. In Romance countries, the vernaculars were still close enough to Latin for many people to get the gist of the Scripture texts (more on this below, in chapter 6, pp. 153–54). Moreover, the stable order of readings for each Sunday and feast day, which was repeated every year, meant that the faithful became more easily familiar with the biblical passages in the course of time.

The Church's Way of Praying

The last passage to be discussed in this chapter is from the *Commentary on the First Letter to Timothy.* The exhortation of 1 Timothy 2:1, "I urge that supplications, prayers, intercessions, and thanksgivings [obsecrationes, orationes, postulationes, gratiarum actiones] be made for all men", prompts Aquinas to reflect on the Church's public worship. In this context, he comments on the rhetorical element in prayer ("Et sicut rhetores faciunt, sic et nos in orando debemus facere") and refers to Cassiodorus' definition of prayer as "spoken reason", which he also quotes in the treatise on prayer in the *Summa.*[31] Rhetorical means, which aim at persuasion, are used in prayer, not in order bend the mind of God, but in order to elevate our heart to him. The same argument is offered in the treatise on prayer, where Aquinas argues for the need of vocal prayer.

Paulinum': Critique littéraire", in *L'interpretazione di san Tommaso delle dottrine di san Paolo: Atti della IX Sessione Plenaria, 19–21 giugno 2009* (Doctor communis) (Vatican City: Pontificia Academia Sancti Thomae Aquinatis, 2009), 150–84.

[31] "Dicitur autem oratio quasi oris ratio": II–II, q. 83, a. 1, *resp.*

After having noted the rhetorical character of prayer, Aquinas explains the pattern of the Church's liturgical prayer, which he structures according to the fourfold exhortation from Saint Paul:

> This is the way of praying in the Church of God: *Almighty, everlasting God* (this is the ascent of the mind, which is prayer), *who gives the Church such benefit* (this is the act of thanksgiving), *pray, we beseech* (this is the intercession), *through [our] Lord* (this is the supplication).[32]

In this passage, Aquinas does not quote a specific oration from the Latin liturgical tradition but, rather, presents the classical pattern of the Roman Collect, which has been examined in chapter III (see above pp. 89–101). The Angelic Doctor's familiarity with these characteristics features of the Roman liturgy is also evident from the fact that he applied them masterfully in the prayers he composed for the feast of Corpus Christi,[33] above all in the well-known Collect:

Deus, qui nobis sub sacramento mirabili
passionis tuae memoriam reliquisti,
tribue, quaesumus,
ita nos corporis et sanguinis tui sacra mysteria venerari,
ut redemptionis tuae fructum in nobis iugiter sentiamus.

---

[32] "Unde iste modus orandi est in Ecclesia Dei: *omnipotens sempiterne Deus*, ecce ascensus mentis, qui est oratio, *qui dedisti Ecclesiae tale beneficium*, ecce gratiarum actio, *praesta, quaesumus*, ecce postulatio, *per dominum*, ecce obsecratio": *Super I Tim.*, c. 2, l. 1.

[33] Recent research has confirmed Aquinas as the author of the liturgical texts for Corpus Christi; see Torrell, *Saint Thomas Aquinas*, 1:129–36, and P.-M. Gy, "L'office du Corpus Christi et s. Thomas d'Aquin: État d'une recherche", *Revue des sciences philosophiques et théologiques* 64 (1980), 491–507. Thomas may have given the lectures on 1 Timothy in Rome between 1265 and 1268 and thus only a few years after he composed the Office of Corpus Christi in Orvieto.

O God, who in this wonderful Sacrament
have left us a memorial of your Passion,
grant us, we pray,
so to revere the sacred mysteries of your Body and Blood
that we may always experience in ourselves
the fruits of your redemption.[34]

In conclusion, from the theological perspective of Saint Thomas Aquinas, the use of a sacred language in the liturgy, with its rhetorical forms and its archaic linguistic elements, belongs to the "solemnity" (*solemnitas*) that is observed in the celebration of the sacraments, especially the Most Holy Eucharist.[35] The concept of *solemnitas* is in fact central to Aquinas' understanding of the liturgy as a whole.[36] The German philosopher Josef Pieper proposed a broad definition of "sacred language", which includes signs and gestures as well as the words used in public worship. In a similar way, the English Dominican Aidan Nichols speaks of "the idiom of worship"; both concepts cover more or less the same ground as Aquinas' idea of *solemnitas*.[37] Sacred language (both in the wider and in the narrower sense of the

---

[34] English translation from *Roman Missal* 2011.

[35] III, q. 64, a. 2 ad 1: "Ad primum ergo dicendum quod illa quae aguntur in sacramentis per homines instituta, non sunt de necessitate sacramenti, sed ad quandam solemnitatem, quae adhibetur sacramentis ad excitandam devotionem et reverentiam in his qui sacramenta suscipiunt." See also III, q. 83, a. 4: "Quia in hoc sacramento totum mysterium nostrae salutis comprehenditur, ideo prae ceteris sacramentsi cum maiori solemnitate agitur", and III, q. 66, a. 10, *resp.*, on the ceremonies of the rite of baptism.

[36] Cf. T. A. Becker, "The Role of *Solemnitas* in the Liturgy according to Saint Thomas Aquinas", in Levering and Dauphinais, *Rediscovering Aquinas and the Sacraments*, 114–35.

[37] J. Pieper, *Religionsphilosophische Schriften*, ed. B. Wald, Werke 7 (Hamburg: Felix Meiner, 2000), 477–536; some of Pieper's important contributions are also available in English: *In Search of the Sacred*, trans. L. Krauth (San Francisco: Ignatius Press, 1991); A. Nichols, *Looking at the Liturgy: A*

term) is part of the sacramental rites ordained by the Church, which are directed "according to the wisdom of Christ" (secundum sapientiam Christi).[38]

Critical View of Its Contemporary Form (San Francisco: Ignatius Press, 1996), 87–114.

[38] III, q. 72, a. 12: "Sed contra est usus Ecclesiae, quae a Spiritu Sancto gubernatur.... Et ideo firmiter tenendum est quod ordinationes Ecclesiae dirigantur secundum sapientiam Christi. Et propter hoc certum esse debet ritus quos Ecclesia observat in hoc et in aliis sacramentis, esse convenientes."

VI

LITURGICAL LATIN AND THE VERNACULAR IN THE MODERN AGE

In the course of the Middle Ages, the formation of national languages and cultures in Europe meant that Latin as the language of the liturgy became even more removed from the language of the people. However, it would be an exaggeration to conclude that the use of Latin as a sacred language was a total barrier to an understanding of and participation in the Mass. In the first place, as the (Lutheran) liturgical scholar Frank Senn argues, such a conclusion rests on a narrow understanding of participation that "sees liturgy only as text and limits participation to speaking roles". Senn continues:

> The laity have always found ways to participate in the liturgy, whether it was in their language or not, and they have always derived meaning from the liturgy, whether it was the intended meaning or not. Furthermore, the laity in worship were surrounded by other "vernaculars" than language, not least of which were the church buildings themselves and the liturgical art that decorated them.[1]

[1] F. C. Senn, *The People's Work: A Social History of the Liturgy* (Minneapolis: Fortress Press, 2006), 145.

Senn also notes in passing that the common accusations against Latin in the liturgy have been greatly overstated. This would certainly hold in countries where the vernacular developed from Latin. Augustine Thompson shows in his study of ordinary religious practice in the Italian cities of the High Middle Ages that, contrary to the claim made by heretical groups, such as the Waldensians, there was a basic understanding at least of the meaning conveyed in Latin liturgical texts and that this was so even among the lesser educated, at least if they chose to follow attentively.[2] Historical sources provide a number of telling examples: as a layman and hermit, Francis of Assisi received the inspiration to found the Friars Minor during the celebration of Mass on the feast of Saint Mathias (February 24, 1209), when the apostles' commission to go and preach the Kingdom of Heaven (Mt 10:7–19) was solemnly proclaimed. His grasp of Latin must have been good enough to allow him to be touched to the core by the words of the Gospel. In 1296, a synod in Grado decreed that deacons were not to use melismatic tones in their chanting of the Gospel, because "these impeded the understanding of the hearers and so the devotion in the minds of the faithful is reduced". The elaborate tones were permitted only for the proclamation of the genealogies of Christ on Christmas and Epiphany and for "the first Gospel chanted by a newly ordained deacon".[3] In Italy, the spoken language of the people was still close enough to the Latin that comprehension of liturgical texts was by no means restricted to the educated clergy. Writing about early modern Europe, Peter Burke records that an increasing part

---

[2] A. Thompson, *Cities of God: The Religion of the Italian Communes 1125–1325* (University Park, Pa.: Pennsylvania State University Press, 2005), 239–41.

[3] Quoted after ibid., 240.

of the laity was studying Latin, including the small but growing group of learned women.[4] The cultural impact of the sacred language in everyday speech is also evident from the resonances of liturgical Latin in the vernacular languages of the Romance countries, some of which go back at least to the early modern period.[5]

The use of Latin in this period still provided an example of "diglossia", which means that "it was considered appropriate to use that language in some situations and domains."[6] It was the language of the cultural elites and served to bind together international communities of ideas, above all the Church and the Republic of Letters. Nonetheless, objections to the use of Latin not only in the liturgy but also in other aspects of the Church's life and in public life at large became more widespread in the Renaissance and Reformation periods. The humanists' movement for a return to the

---

[4] See P. Burke, *Languages and Communities in Early Modern Europe: The 2002 Wiles Lectures Given at Queen's University, Belfast* (Cambridge: Cambridge University Press, 2004), 49, where he names "Isotta Nogarola and Laura Cereta in Italy, Caritas Pirckheimer in Germany, Beatriz Galindo, nicknamed 'La Latina', in Spain, and Mildred Cooke".

[5] Burke, *Languages and Communities*, 50–51, provides a few delightful examples: "In the Venetian of Chioggia, for instance, an authoritarian person is nicknamed *potente de sede*, and someone full of himself *un egosum*, derived respectively from the Magnificat, *Deposuit potentes de sede*, and from St John's Gospel 11.25, *Ego sum resurrectio et vita*. Some of the Italian examples are simple borrowings, like *introibo* for 'preamble' or *confiteor* for 'apology'.... Yet other examples express playfulness, irony and mockery, including the mockery of liturgical Latin itself.... A woman regarded as too pious, for instance, was known in the sixteenth century as *una magnificatte*, while shouting was described as 'singing Vespers', *cantare il vespro*." On this subject, see also R. Bracchi, "Il latino liturgico sulla bocca del popolo", in *Il latino e i cristiani: Un bilancio all'inizio del terzo millennio*, ed. E. dal Covolo and M. Sodi, Monumenta Studia Instrumenta Liturgica 17 (Vatican City: Libreria Editrice Vaticana, 2002), 489–507.

[6] Burke, *Languages and Communities*, 43.

purity of Ciceronian Latinity aggravated this situation, because it meant that a "living second language" was discarded in favor of reviving a language that had been truly "dead".[7]

The problem became acute in the sixteenth century, when the Protestant Reformers, in continuity with dissident movements of the later Middle Ages, attacked Latin as a liturgical language. There was also a theological rationale at the root of this critique: the Protestants' idea of divine worship as essentially a proclamation of the Word of God made them conclude that using a language that was not intelligible to the assembly was contrary to the Gospel. Martin Luther was happy to allow for some Latin, as far as it was understood by the people, and this custom was followed for some time in Lutheran communities. John Calvin, on the other hand, categorically rejected the use of Latin in worship.[8]

At the Council of Trent, the question of liturgical language was debated with remarkable depth, and the arguments produced by the Protestant Reformers were considered very seriously.[9] The *Decree on the Sacrifice of the Mass* of the Council's twenty-second session in 1562, resulting from this discussion, contains a carefully worded doctrinal exposition on the subject, stating that it did not seem *expedient* to the Fathers that the Holy Mass should *generally* be celebrated in the vernacular. However, they recognized the value of the texts of the liturgy for the instruction of the faithful in a language that was intelligible to them. Therefore pastors

---

[7] See C. Mohrmann, "The Ever-Recurring Problem of Language in the Church", in *Études sur le latin des chrétiens*, 4 vols., Storia e letteratura, 65, 87, 103, 143 (Rome: Edizioni di Storia e Letteratura, 1961–1977), 4:152, and Burke, *Languages and Communities*, 144–45.

[8] See H. A. P. Schmidt, *Liturgie et langue vulgaire: Le problème de la langue liturgique chez les premiers Réformateurs et au Concile de Trente*, Analecta Gregoriana 53 (Rome: Apud Aedes Unversitatis Gregorianae, 1950), 23–79.

[9] See Schmidt, *Liturgie et langue vulgaire*, 81–198.

and those entrusted with the care of souls should preach frequently about what is read at Mass, especially on Sundays and feast days.[10] Moreover, canon 9 of the same *Decree on the Sacrifice of the Mass* declares anathema anyone who says that *only* the vernacular language *must* be used in the celebration of Mass; again, the subtle wording of this conciliar text is to be noted.[11]

The question of Latin and the vernacular in the Church's liturgy continued to be discussed in the centuries after Trent, especially in the Catholic Enlightenment of the eighteenth and early nineteenth century, and it came to the fore in the twentieth century.[12] The process of liturgical reform initiated by Pope Pius XII included concessions for several countries to use the vernacular in the administration of sacraments and sacramentals.[13]

The Fathers of the Second Vatican Council addressed the question of the language of worship in a comprehensive

---

[10] Council of Trent, 22nd Session (September 17, 1562), *Decree on the Sacrifice of the Mass*, chap. 8: "Etsi missa magnam contineat populi fidelis eruditionem, non tamen expedire visum est patribus, ut vulgari passim lingua celebraretur. . . ."

[11] Ibid., canon 9: "Si quis dixerit, Ecclesiae Romanae ritum, quo submissa voce pars canonis et verba consecrationis proferuntur, damnandum esse; aut lingua tantum vulgari Missam celebrari debere; aut aquam non miscendam esse vino in calice offerendo, eo quod sit contra Christi institutionem: anathema sit."

[12] Much useful material is assembled in K. Pecklers, *Dynamic Equivalence: The Living Language of Christian Worship*, (Collegeville: Liturgical Press, 2003); see also W. Trapp, *Vorgeschichte und Ursprung der liturgischen Bewegung vorwiegend in Hinsicht auf das deutsche Sprachgebiet* (1940; repr., Münster: Antiquariat Stenderhoff, 1979).

[13] See, for instance, the *Collectio rituum ad instar appendicis Ritualis Romani: Pro omnibus Germaniae dioecesibus: A Sancta Sede approbata* (Regensburg: Pustet, 1950), and *The Small Ritual: Being Extracts from Ordo administrandi sacramenta with an Authorized English Version* (London: Burns and Oates, 1956).

way and granted a significant extension of the use of the vernacular in the Catholic liturgy. The primary motive for this was to promote "fully conscious and active participation" of the people in the liturgy.[14] The relevant article of the Constitution on the Sacred Liturgy *Sacrosanctum concilium*, no. 36, strikes a balance that was reached after some debate on the Council floor, asserting in the first paragraph that "the use of the Latin language is to be preserved in the Latin rites" (§ 1), and then, secondly, granting that the use of the vernacular may be extended, which "will apply in the first place to the readings and directives, and to some of the prayers and chants" (§ 2). Thirdly, "the competent territorial ecclesiastical authority", which ordinarily would be the conference of bishops, is to decide "whether, and to what extent, the vernacular language is to be used" (§ 3). Article 54 of *Sacrosanctum concilium* specifies that in "Masses which are celebrated with the people, a suitable place may be allotted to their mother tongue. This is to apply in the first place to the readings and 'the common prayer,' but also, as local conditions may warrant, to those parts which pertain to the people." At the same time, however, "steps should be taken so that the faithful may also be able to say or to sing together in Latin those parts of the Ordinary of the Mass which pertain to them."

It would seem obvious from these articles of *Sacrosanctum concilium* that the Fathers of Vatican II did not envisage a general introduction of the vernacular, let alone a replacement of Latin with the mother tongue as the liturgical language of the Roman rite. Regarding the Divine Office, the Constitution on the Sacred Liturgy stipulated

[14] Second Vatican Council, Constitution on the Sacred Liturgy *Sacrosanctum concilium* (December 4, 1963), no. 14.

in article 101 that the Latin language was to be retained by clerics, although exceptions were possible (§ 1), while the competent superior of institutes of religious, both men who were not priests and women, could grant the use of the Office in the vernacular (§ 2). Moreover, when the Council approved the use of the mother tongue in the Roman liturgy, it made clear that the texts had to be translations of the Latin liturgical books and that these translations had to be approved by the competent territorial ecclesiastical authority (no. 36, § 4).

The postconciliar developments soon went beyond the limited scope of the Council's Constitution on the Sacred Liturgy, and, as a matter of fact, the vernacular liturgy gradually *replaced* the Latin liturgy. Among the landmarks in this process was Pope Paul VI's Motu Proprio *Sacram liturgiam* of January 25, 1964, just one and a half months after the promulgation of *Sacrosanctum concilium*. With this document, Paul VI permitted the use of the vernacular instead of Latin in the recitation of the hours. He also determined that the translated version should be drawn up and approved by the conferences of bishops and submitted to the Holy See for due approval, that is, confirmation.[15]

The Question of Translation

In the same year, on September 26, 1964, the Consilium for Implementing the Council's Constitution on the Sacred Liturgy issued the instruction *Inter oecumenici*, which came into effect on March 7, 1965 (the First Sunday in Lent) and provided

[15] Paul VI, Apostolic Letter *Sacram liturgiam* given Motu Proprio (January 25, 1964), *Acta Apostolicae Sedis* 56 (1964): 139–44, no. IX.

norms for vernacular translations following *Sacrosanctum concilium*, no. 36, § 3. *Inter oecumenici* made it clear that: (a) "the basis of the translations is the Latin liturgical text"; (b) the work of translation should involve institutes of liturgy or persons who are experts in Scripture, liturgy, the biblical languages, Latin, the vernacular, and music; (c) where applicable, "there should be consultation on translations with bishops of neighboring regions using the same language"; (d) "in nations of several languages there should be a translation for each language"; and, finally, "special attention should be given to the high quality of books used for reading the liturgical text to the people in the vernacular." [16]

Inter oecumenici allowed the use of the vernacular, with reference to *Sacrosanctum concilium*, no. 54, for "Masses, whether sung or recited, celebrated with a congregation": (a) "the proclaiming of the lessons, epistle, and gospel; the universal prayer or prayer of the faithful"; (b) "as befits the circumstances of the place, the chants of the Ordinary of the Mass, namely, the *Kyrie, Gloria, Credo, Sanctus-Benedictus, Agnus Dei*, as well as the introit, offertory, and communion antiphons and the chants between the readings"; (c) "acclamations, greeting, and dialogue formularies, the *Ecce Agnus Dei, Domine, non sum dignus, Corpus Christi* at the communion of the faithful, and the Lord's Prayer with its introduction and embolism". The Canon of the Mass was to remain in Latin.[17] Moreover, the instruction stipulated: "Missals to be used in

[16] Sacred Congregation of Rites, Instruction for the Right Implementation of the Constitution on the Sacred Liturgy *Inter oecumenici* (September 26, 1964), *Acta Apostolicae Sedis* 56 (1964): 877–900, no. 40; English translation in *Documents on the Liturgy 1963–1979: Conciliar, Papal, and Curial Texts* (Collegeville, Minn.: Liturgical Press, 1982), 96.

[17] Conferences of Bishops were authorized to grant the use of the vernacular for the Canon of the Mass by the Sacred Congregation of Rites' Second Instruction for the Right Implementation of the Constitution on the

the liturgy, however, shall contain besides the vernacular version the Latin text as well."[18]

The directives of *Inter oecumenici*, which also included some modifications of the *Ordo Missae*,[19] guided the preparation of bilingual missals in various (Western) languages. The first of these "interim missals", as they have been called with hindsight, was published and implemented in the United States already on November 29, 1964 (the First Sunday of Advent). Contrary to the directive of *Inter oecumenici*, this edition contained only the English, not the Latin text of those parts that could be used in the vernacular.[20] The many changes this missal introduced, not least of which was the extensive use of English, was experienced as a significant rupture in the liturgical life of the Catholic Church.[21]

In an address to translators of liturgical texts given on November 10, 1965, Paul VI presented the basic principles of liturgical translations. The Pope emphasized that trans-

---

Sacred Liturgy *Tres abhinc annos* (May 4, 1967), *Acta Apostolicae Sedis* 59 (1967): 442–48, no. 28.

[18] *Inter oecumenici*, no. 57; English translation: *Documents on the Liturgy*, 101–3.

[19] Ibid., no. 48; English translation: *Documents on the Liturgy*, 98. The *editio typica* of the revised *Ordo Missae* was published on January 27, 1965; cf. *Notitiae* 1 (1965): 101–2.

[20] *Roman Missal: Missale Romanum ex decreto Sacrosancti Concilii Tridentini restitutum Summorum Pontificum cura recognitum cum versionibus lingua anglica exaratis et a coetu episcoporum Civitatum Foederatum America Septentrionalis rite approbatis actis ab Apostolica Sede confirmatis* (New York: Benziger, 1964). This matter was rectified in the 1966 edition, which had the pertinent parts in Latin and English.

[21] See the instructive article of S. Benofy, "The Day the Mass Changed", *Adoremus Bulletin, Online Edition* 15, 10 (February 2010) and 16, 1 (March 2010): http://www.adoremus.org/0210Benofy.html and http://www.adoremus.org/0310Benofy.html (accessed on July 31, 2011). Cf. J. M. O'Toole, *The Faithful: A History of Catholics in America* (Cambridge, Mass.: Belknap Press, 2008), 204 and 208.

lations of liturgical texts "have become part of the rites themselves", unlike previous translations for the use of the faithful, and that for this reason they need to be approved by the local authority and confirmed by the Holy See for liturgical use. The type of language to be used in the liturgy "should always be worthy of the noble realities it signifies, set apart from the everyday speech of the street and the marketplace". This requires that translators "know both Christian Latin and their own modern language", and, since the liturgy should above all be chanted, the translated prayers need to be constructed in such a way that they can be sung according to the rules of music that obtain in different cultures. The challenge for translators is to "make also clarity of language and dignity of expression shine forth in the vernacular translations of liturgical texts".[22]

The question of translation presented itself with greater urgency when in 1969/1970 the new, substantially changed *editio typica* of the *Missale Romanum* was released. The key document guiding the translations of the new liturgical books was the instruction of the Consilium *Comme le prévoit* of January 25, 1969. This instruction shows a few formal irregularities: it was published in six major languages, but not in Latin, the official language of the Holy See; moreover, it bears no official signature, and it was not published in the *Acta Apostolicae Sedis*, the official organ of the Holy See.[23] *Comme le prévoit* is in many ways an elaboration of the above-mentioned address of Paul VI in 1965. However, it introduces

---

[22] Paul VI, *Address to Translators of Liturgical Texts* (November 10, 1965), *Acta Apostolicae Sedis* 57 (1965): 967–70; English translation: *Documents on the Liturgy*, 273 and 274.

[23] Consilium, Instruction on the Translation of Liturgical Texts for Celebrations with a Congregation *Comme le prévoit* (January 25, 1969), *Notitiae* 5 (1969): 3–12.

significant novelties in the methodology of translation: only "some euchological and sacramental formularies", above all the Eucharistic Prayers and the Prefaces, "should be translated integrally and faithfully, without variations, omissions, or insertions".[24] The other prayers of the Mass, which come from the ancient Roman tradition, "may need to be rendered somewhat more freely while conserving the original ideas. This can be done by moderately amplifying them or, if necessary, paraphrasing expressions in order to concretize them for the celebration and the needs of today."[25] Thus *Comme le prévoit* endorsed a hermeneutic of translation known as "dynamic equivalence". This theory was developed by Eugene Nida for the purpose of biblical translation and intended to offer new ways of solving the complex problems that are usually encountered in this work.[26] A word-by-word translation from the source language into the receptor language often does not make sense and fails to communicate the message of the text. This difficulty is felt particularly when it comes to translating Latin liturgical texts, many of which stem from late antiquity, into contemporary languages. Any translation must naturally aim at translating the spiritual and doctrinal content of these ancient prayers in a way that renders justice to the rules and conventions of the receptor language.

However, the theory of "dynamic equivalence" goes much farther, in that it abstracts the content of the text from its linguistic and cultural form and no longer aims at a translation that would reproduce the formal structure of the original

---

[24] *Comme le prévoit*, no. 33; English translation: *Documents on the Liturgy*, 288.

[25] Ibid., no. 34; English translation: *Documents on the Liturgy*, 288–89.

[26] See E. A. Nida, *Toward a Science of Translating, with Special Reference to Principles and Procedures Involved in Bible Translating* (Leiden: Brill, 1964).

as closely as could reasonably be done in a modern language. Rather, the purpose of this approach is to identify the message contained in the original text apart from its linguistic form, which is considered a mere vesture that can be changed according to different cultural contexts. In the process of translation, a new form is to be created that would possess equivalent qualities through which the original content can be adequately expressed. By means of this new form, the translation intends to create in a reader or audience of the receptor language the same informative and emotive effect that the text in its source language would have had in its original context. Dennis McManus of the *Vox Clara* Committee, which has advised the Holy See's Congregation for Divine Worship and the Discipline of the Sacraments on the new English translation of the *Missale Romanum*, has noted that, according to this translation theory, "the connection between form and meaning is almost completely sacrificed in favor of the immediacy of communicating the meaning derived from a source text." In fact, this raises "several vexed questions", above all, how to determine the meaning of a text in abstraction from its form: "Are there not subjective judgments at play in the translator's estimation, for example, of which 'equivalent forms' will help to create the desired reader-listener response?" [27] This

[27] D. McManus, "Translation Theory in *Liturgiam authenticam*", in *Benedict XVI and the Sacred Liturgy: Proceedings of the First Fota International Liturgy Conference 2008*, ed. N.J. Roy and J.E. Rutherford, Fota Liturgy Series (Dublin: Four Courts Press, 2010), 122. McManus also notes that the philosophical roots of this translation theory lie in logical positivism, which "maintains that all true statements can be reduced to verifiable propositional forms which relate meaning to the reader. In terms of translation theory, such meanings are then re-clothed in 'equivalent forms' and rendered into a target language. This complex process of translation places the primary emphasis on the meaning-response of the reader or hearer of a text, with the result that a

methodology guided the translation of the new liturgical books into the vernacular and was applied in the most radical manner to the English-language edition of the *Missale Romanum* of Paul VI, which was prepared by the International Commission on English in the Liturgy (ICEL) and officially approved in 1973.

From a sociolinguistic perspective, the shift from Latin to the vernacular has been described as a "revolution" that has altered "the perceived distinctiveness of liturgical language".[28] A distinction needs to be made here: the first step was to replace—not *de iure* but *de facto*—the Roman Church's language of worship that went back more than 1,500 years with local languages. It was another step to adopt for liturgical translation an idiom that was conceived as following everyday common usage. This tendency was carried farthest in the case of English. There are elements of religious language that are shared by various Christian traditions in the Anglophone world and that were deliberately avoided in the 1973 translation; to name a few examples:[29]

—archaic grammatical forms, such as "thee" and "thou", especially in addressing God;

—vocative syntax structures, such as the classical form of the Collect: "O God, who ...", sometimes also with an adjective: "Almighty and merciful God, who ...";

---

translation is considered a failure if the derived meaning of the source text is not communicated immediately, rather than through some linguistic mediation, in the text of the target language."

[28] D. Crystal, "Liturgical Language in a Sociolinguistic Perspective", in *Language and the Worship of the Church*, ed. D. Jasper and R. C. D. Jasper, Studies in Literature and Religion (Basingstoke: Macmillan, 1990), 122.

[29] These examples are taken from Crystal, "Liturgical Language", 122–23.

— special vocabulary, such as "behold", "vouchsafe", "brethren".

These grammatical features were no longer used in ordinary language, even in a formal register, and had thus acquired a specifically religious character. In the English translation of the *Missale Romanum*, most of these forms were deliberately excluded. Only the specific vocabulary distinguishes the prayer texts as religious discourse, but even here traditional vernacular expressions have been toned down in an attempt to accommodate contemporary use. Inevitably, the doctrinal content was changed as well. A good example of this tendency is the translation of the Opening Prayer for the Eleventh Sunday in Ordinary Time (the prayer is a very slightly modified version of the Collect for the First Sunday after Pentecost in the *Missale Romanum* of 1570–1962):

Missale Romanum 1970
Deus, in te sperantium fortitudo,
invocationibus nostris adesto propitius,
et, quia sine te nihil potest mortalis infirmitas,
gratiae tuae praesta semper auxilium,
ut, in exsequendis mandatis tuis,
et voluntate tibi et actione placeamus.

Missale Romanum 1966
O God, the strength of all who place their trust in you,
graciously hear our prayers.
Because of our weak human nature
we can do nothing without you.
Help us by your grace
that we may fulfill your commands
and please you in will and in action.

ICEL 1973 (*Roman Missal* 1974)
Almighty God,
our hope and our strength,
without you we falter.
Help us to follow Christ and to live according to your will.

The comparison with the "interim missal" of 1966,[30] the first translation of the prayer for liturgical use, makes evident the different hermeneutic of translation. In the 1973 version, the thoroughly biblical[31] appositional phrase that accompanies the simple invocation "O God", "strength of those who hope in you", is rendered blandly, with "hope" and "strength" being simply juxtaposed. The petition "graciously be attentive to our pleas" is omitted. The sense of human frailty, caused by original sin, which gives rises to the insight that without God nothing can be achieved, is greatly weakened. The working of divine grace is reduced to a mere "help", and the desired result, that we may please God in will and in deed by observing his commandments, is turned into a following of Christ (not mentioned at all in the Latin) and a generic living according to God's will.[32]

---

[30] *English-Latin Roman Missal for the United States of America: Containing the Mass Text from the Roman Missal and the Prayers of the Celebrant together with the Ordinary of the Mass from the English-Latin Sacramentary; English Translations Approved by the National Conference of Bishops of the United States of America and Confirmed by the Apostolic See* (New York: Benziger Brothers, 1966).

[31] Cf. Psalm 30[31]:4, where the psalmist calls upon the Lord with the words "fortitudo mea".

[32] Such problems have been specifically mentioned by the Congregation for Divine Worship and the Discipline of the Sacraments, Fifth Instruction for the Right Implementation of the Constitution on the Sacred Liturgy *Liturgiam authenticam* (March 28, 2001), *Acta Apostolicae Sedis* 93 (2001): 685–726, no. 54: "To be avoided in translations is any psychologizing tendency, especially a tendency to replace words treating of the theological virtues by others expressing merely human emotions. As regards words or expressions

Moreover, the English prayer does not provide a grammatical link between the statement of fact and the petition; the consequent staccato tone fails to communicate the rhetorical force of the original.[33] Thus the 1973 ICEL version can hardly be considered more than a paraphrase and does not give justice to the profound and nuanced contents of the original prayer.[34] As Eamon Duffy commented, "a magnificently balanced Augustinian meditation on the dialectic of grace and obedience becomes a vague and semi-Pelagian petition for help in case we falter."[35]

In the course of the years when this translation was in use, its deficiencies became apparent both on a pastoral and

---

conveying a properly divine notion of causality (e.g., those expressed in Latin by the words '*praesta, ut* ...'), one should avoid employing words or expressions denoting a merely extrinsic or profane sort of assistance instead."

[33] Cf. the rhetorical analysis of this prayer by M. G. Haessly, *Rhetoric in the Sunday Collects of the Roman Missal: With Introduction, Text, Commentary and Translation* (Cleveland: Ursuline College for Women, 1938), 73–75.

[34] The ICEL translation of 2010 (*Roman Missal* 2011) is an absolute improvement on the 1973 version and also compares well with the 1966 prayer:

> O God, strength of those who hope in you,
> graciously hear our pleas,
> and since without you mortal frailty can do nothing,
> grant us always the help of your grace,
> that in following your commands
> we may please you by our resolve and our deeds.

[35] E. Duffy, "The Catholic Church on the Eve of the New Millennium", *Catholic Medical Quarterly* 50 (2000): 42–47, and 51 (2001): 32, also available at: http://www.christendom-awake.org/pages/duffy/newmill.html (accessed on August 11, 2011). Similar problems exist in the German translation of 1975, though not on the same scale; cf. N. Lohfink, "Liturgische Bibelverdunstung: Die Bibel-Intertextualität bei der Verdeutschung der lateinischen Liturgie", *Stimmen der Zeit* 218 (2000): 247–59; J. Ratzinger, "Um die Erneuerung der Liturgie: Antwort auf Reiner Kaczynski", *Stimmen der Zeit* 219 (2001): 837–43; and A. Stock, *Liturgie und Poesie: Zur Sprache des Gottesdienstes* (Kevelaer: Butzon & Bercker, 2010).

on a scholarly level.[36] The urgency to remedy this situation was recognized by the Holy See, and *Comme le prévoit* was replaced by the instruction *Liturgiam authenticam* of the Congregation for Divine Worship and the Discipline of the Sacraments in 2001. It is the Fifth Instruction for the correct implementation of the Council's Constitution on the Sacred Liturgy and thus stands on a par with the first one in this series, the momentous *Inter oecumenici* of 1964. With *Liturgiam authenticam*, previous norms on the translation of liturgical texts are superseded, with the exception of those presented in the Fourth Instruction *Varietates legitimae* of 1994 concerning difficult questions on the Roman liturgy and inculturation.[37] According to *Liturgiam authenticam*, all translations of liturgical books in use since the Second Vatican Council are to be examined and revised. In order to assure that the translations are authentic and correspond with the original texts, they need the *recognitio* of the Apostolic See, a concept dating from Pope Sixtus V (1585–1590) and his reform of the Roman Curia. The *recognitio* of legal or liturgical texts goes beyond a generic approval and includes a careful and detailed examination of whether the universal norms have been correctly applied. Hence the term should be translated, not as "authorization", but rather as "review".[38]

---

[36] See, for instance, the pertinent critique of E. Duffy, "Rewriting the Liturgy: The Theological Implications of Translation", in *Beyond the Prosaic: Renewing the Liturgical Movement*, ed. S. Caldecott (Edinburgh: T&T Clark, 1998), 97–126.

[37] Congregation for Divine Worship and the Discipline of the Sacraments, Fourth Instruction for the Right Implementation of the Constitution on the Sacred Liturgy *Varietates legitimae* (January 25, 1994), *Acta Apostolicae Sedis* 87 (1995): 288–314.

[38] See Pontifical Council for Legislative Texts, "Nota Esplicativa X: La natura giuridica e l'estensione della 'recognitio' della Santa Sede", *Communicationes* 38 (2006): 10–11.

In the process of reviewing the translations presented by conferences of bishops, the Congregation of Divine Worship and the Discipline of the Sacraments can introduce even substantial modifications.[39]

Liturgiam authenticam is an important document of considerable length that deals with the translation and publication of liturgical books in the vernacular in a comprehensive way. This is not the place to provide a complete analysis of its rich and nuanced contents; instead, I intend to highlight a few aspects of it, which I consider most relevant for the argument of this chapter. The instruction notes that the rich spiritual and doctrinal patrimony that is contained in the Latin liturgical texts of the Roman rite is to be preserved and passed on through the centuries. In order to achieve this goal, "it is to be kept in mind from the beginning that the translation of the liturgical texts of the Roman Liturgy is not so much a work of creative innovation as it is of rendering the original texts faithfully and accurately into the vernacular language." The different methodology that this instruction requires of translators is made very clear: "While it is permissible to arrange the wording, the syntax and the style in such a way as to prepare a flowing vernacular text suitable to the rhythm of popular prayer, the original text, insofar as possible, must be translated integrally and in the most exact manner, without omissions or additions in terms of their content, and without paraphrases or glosses. Any adaptation to the characteristics or the nature of the various vernacular languages is to be sober and discreet."[40]

---

[39] See *Liturgiam authenticam*, no. 80; cf. *Code of Canon Law*, can. 838, §1.

[40] *Liturgiam authenticam*, no. 20.

The content of the liturgical texts should be "evident and comprehensible even to the faithful who lack any special intellectual formation"; for this reason "the translations should be characterized by a kind of language which is easily understandable." At the same time, however, liturgical translations need to preserve the "dignity, beauty, and doctrinal precision" of the original text. The aim set for liturgical translation is indeed a high one: "By means of words of praise and adoration that foster reverence and gratitude in the face of God's majesty, his power, his mercy and his transcendent nature, the translations will respond to the hunger and thirst for the living God that is experienced by the people of our own time, while contributing also to the dignity and beauty of the liturgical celebration itself."[41]

The instruction also addresses the often poorly understood question of inculturation in a reflected and balanced way. Liturgical translation should communicate the Church's perennial treasury of prayer "by means of language understandable in the cultural context for which it is intended"; however,

> it should also be guided by the conviction that liturgical prayer not only is formed by the genius of a culture, but itself contributes to the development of that culture. Consequently it should cause no surprise that such language differs somewhat from ordinary speech. Liturgical translation that takes due account of the authority and integral content of the original texts will facilitate the development of a sacral vernacular, characterized by a vocabulary, syntax and grammar that are proper to divine worship, even though it is not to be excluded that it may exercise an influence

---

[41] Ibid., no. 25.

even on everyday speech, as has occurred in the languages of peoples evangelized long ago.[42]

This important passage shows an awareness of the complex relationship between faith and culture that takes account of the characteristics of "sacred language" in the Christian tradition, questions that have been addressed in the first and second chapter of this book.

When reading *Liturgiam authenticam*, one cannot but be impressed by the high standards that are demanded for the translation of liturgical texts. No doubt, translation is a difficult undertaking, and it is made even more arduous by the particular nature of the texts in question. The task of reproducing the beauty and dignity of the Canon of the Mass or the ancient orations of the *Missale Romanum* in the vernacular would require translators as gifted in their mother tongue as Miles Coverdale or Thomas Cranmer were in the sixteenth century. None other than Martin Luther wrote that one would need poets to create a popular liturgy.[43] Nonetheless, the criteria of *Liturgiam authenticam* rest on solid philological, historical, and theological foundations and are eminently suitable for the critical revision of the postconciliar translations, which were produced under great pressure of time and not rarely approved without a due process of examination and revision. According to McManus, the most important aspect of the instruction from the point of view of translation theory is the claim "that the Church possesses full authority to self-interpret her own liturgical texts and, furthermore, that in so doing, she best captures

[42] Ibid., no. 47.

[43] M. Luther, *Formula Missae et Communionis* (1523), Weimarer Ausgabe, 12:218.

her own authorial intent within 'formal equivalency' translation".[44]

A Tale of Two Translations

The first fruit of *Liturgiam authenticam* in the English-speaking world is the new, thoroughly revised translation of the *Missale Romanum* according to the third *editio typica.*[45] After the liturgical texts had been prepared and approved by various Anglophone conferences of bishops all over the world, in a long and at times arduous process, the Holy See gave its *recognitio* in March 2010. The new *Roman Missal* has been implemented in most English-speaking countries in the course of the year 2011.

There are many changes in the liturgical texts that concern not only the celebrant priests themselves, but all the faithful, most notably the people's response to the liturgical greeting "The Lord be with you" (for "Dominus vobiscum"), which will no longer be "And also with you", but "And with your spirit" (for "Et cum spiritu tuo").[46] Moreover, the translation of the *Ordo Missae* has been systematically reworked, following the criteria of *Liturgiam authenticam.* The introduction of the new translation is accompanied by many initiatives and publications to explain its rationale and to provide extensive commentary on the text. Here a brief

---

[44] McManus, "Translation Theory", 129.

[45] *Missale Romanum ex decreto Sacrosancti Oecumenici Concilii Vaticani II instauratum auctoritate Pauli PP. VI promulgatum Ioannis Pauli PP. II cura recognitum,* editio typica tertia, (Vatican City: Typis Vaticanis, 2002). An emended reprint of this edition was published in 2008.

[46] An overdue correction: cf. the compelling article by B. Botte, "Dominus vobiscum", *Bible et vie chrétienne* 62 (1965): 33–38.

discussion of a few selected passages will suffice to show the characteristics of the new version in comparison to the older one of 1973.[47]

The first set of passages is taken from the First Eucharistic Prayer, the Roman Canon. In Latin prose texts, the placing of the various parts of a sentence can be very significant. The Post-Sanctus part of the Canon begins with the striking form of address "Te igitur, clementissime Pater". The 1973 version renders this rather blandly as "We come to you, Father"; thus the emphasis has already shifted from God the Father, to whom the prayer is addressed, to our action ("we come"). By contrast, the new translation is faithful to the unusual beginning of the Latin prayer with "To you, therefore, most merciful Father". The force of the Latin *igitur* has long been debated among liturgists; it has been argued that this refers back to the Preface, in which we thank and praise God for his wonderful work of salvation. Since the *Sanctus* came in at a later stage in the development of the liturgy, it would seem plausible that *igitur* originally connected the petition to make our offering acceptable to the initial act of praise; however, it can now be construed to take up the acclamation of the *Benedictus*: "Blessed is he who comes in the name of the Lord. Hosanna in the highest." Note that the new translation has the superlative "most merciful Father" as in the Latin. Moreover, while the 1973 version leaves out "Dominum nostrum", the phrase is now rendered integrally: "through Jesus Christ, your Son, our Lord".

The choice of the earlier version "We come to you ... with praise and thanksgiving ... we ask you" is curious, because the Latin Canon only reads "supplices rogamus ac

---

[47] As found in *Roman Missal* 1974.

petimus" at this point. Eamon Duffy suggested that this would reflect an opinion current among liturgists in the postconciliar period that the Roman Canon was somehow deficient because it gave priority to the elements of petition and intercession over those of praise and thanksgiving. The translators may have tried to remedy this by letting the prayer begin with the words they chose.[48] Be that as it may, the 1973 version does not take into account the formula "rogamus ac petimus", which is characteristic of Roman euchological style. Here we observe the typical use of consecutive synonyms or near-synonyms. The doubling of the verb increases the force and intensity of the expression. In the 2010 version, this is translated as "we make humble prayer and petition."

There are other examples of the use of near-synonyms, such as "accepta habeas et benedicas" (translated in both versions as "accept and bless") and "haec dona, haec munera, haec sancta sacrificia illibata". In this latter phrase, there is an impressive climax from the simple expression of "gifts" to a word that implies "what is due" and can literally mean "tributes", "sacrifices". The 1973 version opts for a more paraphrastic translation ("these gifts we offer you in sacrifice"), not communicating the idea that these sacrifices are indeed *sancta* and *illibata*, whereas the 2010 version does justice to the three different terms and also reproduces the rhetorical movement of the phrase in English: "these gifts, these offerings, these holy and unblemished sacrifices".

In the Anamnesis prayer after the Consecration *Unde et memores*, there are several outstanding stylistic features, above all in the clause "offerimus tibi . . .". The asyndeton "hostiam puram, hostiam sanctam, hostiam immaculatam", with

[48] Duffy, "Rewriting the Liturgy", 102.

three near-synonymous adjectives, is once again characteristic of Roman prayer style. Whereas the 1973 translation reduces this to "this holy and perfect sacrifice", the 2010 version retains the original's rhetorical force: "this pure victim, this holy victim, this spotless victim". In the older version, there is a remarkable tendency to leave out certain qualifying adjectives: "beatae passionis" is rendered as "his passion" (new: "the blessed Passion"), "in caelos gloriosae ascensionis" as "his ascension into glory" (new: "the glorious Ascension into heaven"), "plebs tua sancta" as "your people" (new: "your holy people"), and "Panem sanctum vitae aeternae" as "the bread of life" (new: "the holy Bread of eternal life"). In this prayer there is also an example of the earlier translators' decision to change the respective forms of address for God used in the prayers of the Roman rite (Deus; Domine; Pater; Domine, Deus noster; Omnipotens aeterne Deus, and so on). There are many examples of this decision in the Collects of the Missal. In the *Unde et memores* prayer, *Domine* was translated as "Father", no doubt to highlight the fact that this prayer is addressed to the God the Father, while shortly before in the Memorial Acclamation and shortly afterward, *Dominus* is used to refer to the Son. However, it would seem that in the original Canon *Dominus* is used deliberately for both the Father and the Son to underline that both are "Lord" and thus equal in divinity. Moreover, in the context of the prayer, it is clear that the address "Domine" refers to the Father, whereas "Domini nostri" (left out in the earlier version) means Christ, his Son.

As briefly discussed above, the variable prayers of the Mass in the 1973 ICEL translation are particularly problematic, because *Comme le prévoit* dispensed from the need to translate the texts literally and integrally. Hence it is in the Collects of the Mass where the difference between the two versions is most obvious and where the improvements of the new *Roman Missal* are most remarkable. My example is the Collect for the Twenty-First Sunday in Ordinary Time (also for Monday of the Fifth Week of Easter; in the *Missale Romanum* 1570–1962, it is the Collect for the Fourth Sunday after Easter):

> *Missale Romanum* 1970–2008
> Deus, qui fidelium mentes unius efficis voluntatis,
> da populis tuis id amare quod praecipis,
> id desiderare quod promittis,
> ut, inter mundanas varietates,
> ibi nostra fixa sint corda, ubi vera sunt gaudia.
>
> ICEL 1973 (*Roman Missal* 1974)
> Father,
> help us to seek the values
> that will bring us lasting joy
> in this changing world.
> In our desire for what you promise
> make us one in mind and heart.
>
> ICEL 2010 (*Roman Missal* 2011)
> O God, who cause the minds of the faithful
> to unite in a single purpose,
> grant your people to love what you command
> and to desire what you promise,
> that, amid the uncertainties of this world,
> our hearts may be fixed on that place
> where true gladness is found.

The 1973 English version rearranges the structure of the Latin prayer: the *statement of fact* at the beginning, namely, that God effects unity of will among the faithful, appears as a *petition* at the end of the prayer. On the other hand, the plea that God may grant the desire for his promises is turned into a phrase that describes the condition of those who make the prayer. Thus the carefully crafted sequence of ideas and their rhetorical expression, which are so characteristic of classical Roman orations, are largely disregarded. There are further problems: the proper form of address is not respected, because "Father" is not a translation of *Deus*; whereas in the Latin the petition is made on behalf of "populis tuis", that is, the entire people of God, the older version restricts this to an undetermined "us", which is presumably identified with the individual worshipping community, and so narrows the ecclesiological scope of the prayer. Even though the Latin text later shifts to "our hearts", when the desired result is expressed, the initial request is of a wider nature. The actual rendering of the petition is highly questionable: "help us . . ." introduces a feeble notion of divine causality and smacks of semi-Pelagianism. Equally problematic is "seek the values . . ." in place of "love what you command and desire what you promise". Reducing the concretely biblical concept of love for God's law and a longing for his promises to "values" can only be described as a step toward self-secularization and possibly even moral relativism (insofar as "values" is a term that is commonly used to replace discussions of an objective moral order). The mysterious working of divine grace in the human heart, which the Latin prayer expresses in strongly Augustinian terms, is lost in translation. If one asks of what kind these "values" are, the answer is: those "that will bring us lasting joy in this changing world". It should be noted that "inter mundanas varietates" has negative connotations that are not captured by the insipid phrase "changing world". More importantly, however, the original text does precisely *not* ask for lasting joy amid the uncertainties of *this* world; rather, it asks that our hearts should be anchored in that place where true joy is found: the transcendent reality of heaven. One can easily hear the echo of Luke 12:34: "For where your treasure is, there will your heart be also."

It is hard, therefore, to avoid the conclusion that the 1973 ICEL version turns the sense of the Latin prayer upside down. This is evident from the comparison with the 2010 ICEL version, which faithfully renders the original's sequence of ideas and succeeds in presenting them integrally. Of course, even the best translation can only approximate the elegance of the Latin oration,[49] with its prose rhythm and its rhetorical elements, such as the parallel construction "id amare quod praecipis" (*cursus tardus*)—"id desiderare quod promittis" (*cursus trispondiacus*), with the use of assonance and alliteration. This graceful composition both relates and distinguishes the precepts and the promises of God.

In conclusion, unlike its predecessor, the 2010 ICEL version makes the treasury of the Latin liturgical tradition available to the Church in the English-speaking world. It also contributes greatly to the formation of a "sacral vernacular", as envisaged by *Liturgiam authenticam*: an idiom of worship that is distinguished from everyday speech and is experienced as the voice of the Church at prayer.[50] For the pastors who are entrusted with the task of introducing the new edition of the *Roman Missal* to their communities, this is also a unique opportunity for teaching the Catholic faith that finds a beautiful and profound expression in these

---

[49] Cf. Haessly, *Rhetoric in the Sunday Collects*, 65–68.

[50] *Liturgiam authenticam*, no. 27, also observes in this context: "These principles, in fact, should free the Liturgy from the necessity of frequent revisions when modes of expression may have passed out of popular usage."

prayers.[51] The revised translation, which represents an important step in the ongoing process of liturgical renewal desired by the Second Vatican Council, can also be considered a major contribution to what then-Cardinal Joseph Ratzinger called "reform of the reform".[52]

At the same time, every effort should be made to foster and, indeed, to revive the use of Latin in the liturgy. As has already been noted in the introduction to this book, such is the intention of the Second Vatican Council's Constitution on the Sacred Liturgy and of the Magisterium of the recent popes (see above, pp. 11–13). In an epoch marked by unprecedented mobility and globalization, this common liturgical language is "a manifest and beautiful sign of unity, as well as an effective antidote for any corruption of doctrinal truth", as Pius XII observed at a time when its use had already been contested.[53] The linguistic fragmentation of Catholic worship in the postconciliar period has gone so far that the majority of the faithful today can hardly pray the *Pater noster* together when they gather at international meetings in Rome or Lourdes. Nevertheless, the question of sacred language touches on the very essence of the rite, which then-Cardinal

---

[51] The introduction of the new translation has been accompanied by many publications and intiatives. Here I would just like to single out one book, which serves as the basis for a program of formation: C. Carstens and D. Martis, *Mystical Body, Mystical Voice: Encountering Christ in the Words of the Mass* (Chicago: Liturgy Training Publications, 2011).

[52] See, above all, his résumé of the important 2001 Fontgombault meeting: "Bilan et Perspectives", in Ratzinger, *Theologie der Liturgie: Die sakramentale Begründung christlicher Existenz*, Gesammelte Schriften 11 (Freiburg: Herder 2008), 657–82, esp. 673–77. English translation in *Looking Again at the Question of the Liturgy with Cardinal Ratzinger: Proceedings of the 2001 Fontgombault Liturgical Conference*, ed. A. Reid (Farnborough: Saint Michael's Abbey Press, 2003), 145–53.

[53] Pius XII, Encyclical on the Sacred Liturgy *Mediator Dei* (November 20, 1947), *Acta Apostolicae Sedis* 39 (1947): 521–95, no. 60.

Ratzinger at one occasion defined as "a condensed form of living Tradition".[54] In his well-known monograph on *The Spirit of the Liturgy*, the present Pontiff also observed:

> The Church does not pray in some kind of mythical omnitemporality. She cannot forsake her roots. She recognizes the true utterance of God precisely in the concreteness of its history, in time and place: to these God ties us, and by these we are all tied together.[55]

[54] J. Ratzinger, "Preface", in *The Organic Development of the Liturgy: The Principles of Liturgical Reform and Their Relation to the Twentieth-Century Liturgical Movement Prior to the Second Vatican Council*, by A. Reid, 2nd ed. (San Francisco: Ignatius Press, 2005), 11.

[55] J. Ratzinger, *The Spirit of the Liturgy*, trans. J. Saward (San Francisco: Ignatius Press, 2000), 164.

BIBLIOGRAPHY

Ancient and medieval sources, which are quoted in the individual chapters of the book according to their current critical editions, are not included in this bibliography.

Agende für evangelisch-lutherische Kirchen und Gemeinden. Vol. 1: *Der Hauptgottesdienst mit Predigt und heiligem Abendmahl und die sonstigen Predigt- und Abendmahlsgottesdienste*. Berlin and Hamburg: Lutherisches Verlagshaus, 1955.

Ashworth, H. "The Influence of the Lombard Invasions on the Gregorian Sacramentary". *Bulletin of the John Rylands Library, Manchester* 37 (1954): 305–27.

______. "The Liturgical Prayers of St Gregory the Great". *Traditio* 15 (1959): 107–61.

Atkinson, C. M. "Missa graeca". In *Messe und Motette*, edited by L. Lütteken, 18–19. MGG prisma. Kassel et al.: Bärenreiter et al., 2002.

Auerbach, E. *Literatursprache und Publikum in der lateinischen Spätantike und im Mittelalter*. Bern: Francke, 1958.

Bagatti, B. "L'origine gerosolimitana della preghiera Supra quae del Canone Romano". *Bibbia e Oriente* 21 (1979): 101–8.

Banniard, M. *Viva voce: Communication écrite et communication orale du IVe au IXe siècle en occident latin*. Collection des études augustiniennes. Série Moyen-âge et temps modernes 25. Paris: Institut des études augustiniennes, 1992.

Bardy, G. *La question des langues dans l'Église ancienne*. Études de Théologie Historique. Paris: Beauchesne, 1948.

Barthe, C. "The 'Mystical' Meaning of the Ceremonies of the Mass: Liturgical Exegesis in the Middle Ages". In *The Genius of the Roman Liturgy: Historical Diversity and Spiritual Reach: Proceedings of the 2006 Oxford CIEL Colloquium*, edited by U.M. Lang, 179–97. Chicago: Hillenbrand, 2010.

Bastiaensen, A.A.R. "Die Bibel in den Gebetsformeln der lateinischen Kirche". In *The Impact of Scripture in Early Christianity*, edited by J. den Boeft and M.L. van Poll-van de Lisdonk, 39–57. Supplements to Vigiliae Christianae 44. Leiden, Boston, and Cologne: Brill, 1999.

Bäumer, S. *Geschichte des Breviers: Versuch einer quellenmäßigen Darstellung der Entwicklung des altkirchlichen und des römischen Officiums bis auf unsere Tage*. Freiburg im Breisgau: Herder, 1895. Reprinted, Bonn: nova & vetera, 2004.

Baumstark, A. "Antik-römischer Gebetsstil im Messkanon". In *Miscellanea Liturgica in honorem L. C. Mohlberg*, 1:301–31. Bibliotheca Ephemerides liturgicae 22. Rome: Ed. Liturgiche, 1948.

______. *Liturgie comparée: Principes et méthodes pour l'étude historique des liturgies chrétiennes*. 3rd ed., revised by B. Botte. Collection Irénikon. Chevetogne: Éditions de Chevetogne, 1953.

______. *Missale Romanum: Seine Entwicklung, ihre wichtigsten Urkunden und Probleme*. Eindhoven and Nijmegen: van Eupen, 1929.

______. "Das 'Problem' des römischen Messkanons, eine Retractatio auf geistesgeschichtlichem Hintergrund". *Ephemerides liturgicae* 53 (1939): 204–43.

______. "Ein Übersetzungsfehler im Meßkanon". *Studia catholica* 5 (1928): 378–82.

Becker, T.A. "The Role of *Solemnitas* in the Liturgy according to Saint Thomas Aquinas". In *Rediscovering Aquinas and the*

Sacraments: Studies in Sacramental Theology, edited by M. Levering and M. Dauphinais, 114–35. Chicago: Hillenbrand, 2009.

Bell, C. *Ritual: Perspectives and Dimensions*. New York: Oxford University Press, 1997.

Benedict XVI. *Address to the Clergy of Rome*. Basilica of Saint John Lateran, May 13, 2005; English translation: http://www.vatican.va/holy_father/benedict_xvi/speeches/2005/may/documents/hf_ben-xvi_spe_20050513_roman-clergy_en.html.

———. *Address to the Italian Bishops taking part in the 54th Assembly of the Italian Bishops' Conference*, May 30, 2005; English translation: http://www.vatican.va/holy_father/benedict_xvi/speeches/2005/may/documents/hf_ben-xvi_spe_20050530_cei_en.html.

———. Apostolic Letter *Summorum Pontificum* given Motu Proprio (July 7, 2007). *Acta Apostolicae Sedis* 99 (2007): 777–81; (unofficial) English translation: http://www.catholic-ew.org.uk/content/download/5724/39439/file/Apostolic_Letter_Summorum_Pontificum.pdf.

———. *Faith, Reason and the University: Memories and Reflections: Lecture at the Meeting with the Representatives of Science in the Aula Magna of the University of Regensburg*, September 12, 2006; English translation: http://www.vatican.va/holy_father/benedict_xvi/speeches/2006/september/documents/hf_ben-xvi_spe_20060912_university-regensburg_en.html.

———. Letter to the Bishops on the occasion of the publication of the Apostolic Letter *Summorum Pontificum* given Motu Proprio (July 7, 2007). *Acta Apostolicae Sedis* 99 (2007): 795–99; English translation: http://www.vatican.va/holy_father/benedict_xvi/letters/2007/documents/hf_ben-xvi_let_20070707_lettera-vescovi_en.html.

———. Post-Synodical Apostolic Exhortation *Sacramentum caritatis* (February 22, 2007). *Acta Apostolicae Sedis* 99 (2007): 105–80;

English translation: http://www.vatican.va/holy_father/benedict_xvi/apost_exhortations/documents/hf_ben-xvi_exh_20070222_sacramentum-caritatis_en.html.

______. "Zum Eröffnungsband meiner Schriften". In *Theologie der Liturgie: Die sakramentale Begründung christlicher Existenz*, 5–8. Gesammelte Schriften 11. Freiburg: Herder, 2008.

Benofy, S. "The Day the Mass Changed". *Adoremus Bulletin Online Edition* 15, 10 (February 2010), and 16, 1 (March 2010): http://www.adoremus.org/0210Benofy.html and http://www.adoremus.org/0310Benofy.html.

Berschin, W. *Griechisch-lateinisches Mittelalter: Von Hieronymus zu Nikolaus von Kues*. Bern and Munich: Francke, 1980.

Beumer, J. "Die ältesten Zeugnisse für die römische Eucharistiefeier bei Ambrosius von Mailand". *Zeitschrift für katholische Theologie* 95 (1973): 311–24.

Bishop, E. "The Genius of the Roman Rite". In *Liturgica Historica*, 1–19. Oxford: Clarendon Press, 1918.

______. "Observations on the Liturgy of Narsai". In *The Liturgical Homilies of Narsai*, by R. H. Connolly, 87–163. Texts and Studies 8, 1. Cambridge: Cambridge University Press, 1909.

Blaise, A. *Le vocabulaire latin des principaux thèmes liturgiques*. Revised by A. Dumas. Turnhout: Brepols, 1966.

Botte, B. *Le Canon de la messe romaine*. Textes et études liturgiques 2. Louvain: Abbaye du Mont César, 1935.

______. "Dominus vobiscum". *Bible et vie chrétienne* 62 (1965): 33–38. (A long excerpt in English is now available in *Antiphon* 14 [2010]: 230–35.)

______, and C. Mohrmann. *L'ordinaire de la messe: Texte critique, traduction et études*. Études liturgique 2. Paris: Cerf, and Louvain: Abbaye du Mont César, 1953.

Bouley, A. *From Freedom to Formula: The Evolution of the Eucharistic Prayer from Oral Improvisation to Written Texts*. Studies in Christian Antiquity 21. Washington, D.C.: Catholic University of America Press, 1981.

Bouyer, L. *Eucharist: Theology and Spirituality of the Eucharistic Prayer*. Translated by C. U. Quinn. Notre Dame and London: University of Notre Dame Press, 1968.

Bracchi, R. "Il latino liturgico sulla bocca del popolo". *Il latino e i cristiani: Un bilancio all'inizio del terzo millennio*, edited by E. dal Covolo and M. Sodi, 489–507. Monumenta Studia Instrumenta Liturgica 17. Vatican City: Libreria Editrice Vaticana, 2002.

Bradshaw, P. "The Genius of the Roman Rite Revisited". In *Ever Directed towards the Lord: The Love of God in the Liturgy Past, Present, and Hoped For*, edited by U. M. Lang, 49–61. London: T&T Clark, 2007.

Bradshaw, P. F., M. E. Johnson, and L. E. Philips. *The Apostolic Tradition: A Commentary*. Hermeneia. Minneapolis, Minn.: Fortress Press, 2002.

Brandenburg, H. *Die frühchristlichen Kirchen in Rom*. 2nd ed. Regensburg: Schnell und Steiner, 2005.

Brightman, F. E. *The English Rite: Being a Synopsis of the Sources and Revisions of the Book of Common Prayer with an Introduction and an Appendix*. 2 vols. 2nd ed. 1921; repr., Farnborough: Gregg International, 1970.

______. *Liturgies Eastern and Western*. Vol. 1. Oxford: Clarendon Press, 1896.

Brock, S. P. "Aspects of Translation Technique in Antiquity". *Greek, Roman and Byzantine Studies* 20 (1979): 69–87 (= *Syriac Perspectives on Late Antiquity*. Collected Studies Series 199. London: Variorum Reprints, 1984, no. III).

______. "Diachronic Aspects of Syriac Word Formation: An Aid for Dating Anonymous Texts". In *V. Symposium Syriacum: Katholieke Universiteit, Leuven, 29–31 août 1988*, edited by R. Lavenant, 321–30. Orientalia Christiana Analecta 236. Rome: Pont. Inst. Studiorum Orientalium, 1990.

______. "Gabriel of Qatar's Commentary on the Liturgy". *Hugoye: Journal of Syriac Studies* 6/2 (2003): http://syrcom.cua.edu/Hugoye/Vol6No2/HV6N2Brock.html (accessed August 29, 2011).

Brown, P. *Power and Persuasion in Late Antiquity: Towards a Christian Empire*. Madison: University of Wisconsin Press, 1992.

Bruns, P. "Narses von Edessa". In *Lexikon der antiken christlichen Literatur*, edited by S. Döpp and W. Geerlings, 514–15. 3rd rev. and enlarged ed. Freiburg: Herder, 2002.

Budde, A. "Improvisation im Eucharistiegebet: Zur Technik freien Betens in der Alten Kirche". *Jahrbuch für Antike und Christentum* 44 (2001): 127–44.

Burke, P. *The Art of Conversation*. Ithaca: Cornell University Press, 1993.

______. *Languages and Communities in Early Modern Europe: The 2002 Wiles Lectures given at Queen's University, Belfast*. Cambridge: Cambridge University Press, 2004.

Burton, P. *Language in the* Confessions *of Augustine*. Oxford: Oxford University Press, 2007.

______. *The Old Latin Gospels: A Study of Their Texts and Language*. Oxford Early Christian Studies. Oxford: Oxford University Press, 2000.

Callewaert, C. *S. Léon le Grand et les textes du Léonien*. Extract from *Sacris Erudiri* I, 1948. Bruges: Beyart; La Haye: Nijhoff, 1948.

Cameron, A. "Latin Revival of the Fourth Century". In *Renaissances before the Renaissance: Cultural Revivals of Late Antiquity and the Middle Ages*, edited by W. Treadgold, 42–58. Stanford: Stanford University Press, 1984.

Candler, P. M. "Liturgically Trained Memory: A Reading of *Summa Theologiae* III.83". *Modern Theology* 19 (2004): 423–55.

Capelle, B. "Le Kyrie de la messe et le pape Gélase". *Révue Bénédictine* 46 (1934): 126–44.

______. "La main de S. Grégorie dans le sacramentaire grégorien". *Revue Bénédictine* 49 (1937): 13–28.

______. "Messes du pape s. Gélase dans le sacramentaire de Vérone". In *Travaux liturgiques de doctrine et d'histoire.* Vol. 2: *Histoire: La messe*, 79–105. Louvain: Abbaye du Mont César, 1962.

______. "L'oeuvre liturgique de s. Gélase". In *Travaux liturgiques de doctrine et d'histoire.* Vol. 2. *Histoire: La messe*, 146–60. Louvain: Abbaye du Mont César, 1962.

______. "Retouches gélasiennes dans le sacramentaire de Vérone". In *Travaux liturgiques de doctrine et d'histoire.* Vol. 2: *Histoire: La messe*, 106–15. Louvain: Abbaye du Mont César, 1962.

Caspari, C. P. *Ungedruckte, unbeachtete und wenig beachtete Quellen zur Geschichte des Taufsymbols und der Glaubensregel.* 3 vols. Christiania: Malling, 1866–1875.

Cavallini, S. "Review of C. Mohrmann, *Latin vulgaire, latin des chrétiens, latin medieval*". *Gnomon* 29 (1957): 65–69.

Chavasse, A. "Messes du pape Vigile (537–555) dans le sacramentaire léonien". *Ephemerides Liturgicae* 64 (1950): 161–213, and 66 (1952): 145–215.

Coebergh, C. "S. Gélase Ier, auteur principal de plusieurs messes et prières du sacramentaire léonien". *Ephemerides Liturgicae* 65 (1951): 171–81.

Coleman, R. "Vulgar Latin and the Diversity of Christian Latin". In *Actes du 1er Colloque international sur le latin vulgaire et tardif (Pécs, 2–5 septembre 1985)*, edited by J. Herman, 37–52. Tübingen: Niemeyer, 1987.

Congregation for Divine Worship and the Discipline of the Sacraments, Fifth Instruction for the Right Implementation of the Constitution on the Sacred Liturgy *Liturgiam authenticam* (March 28, 2001). *Acta Apostolicae Sedis* 93 (2001): 685–726. English translation: http://www.vatican.va/roman_curia/congregations/ccdds/documents/rc_con_ccdds_doc_20010507_liturgiam-authenticam_en.html.

______. Fourth Instruction for the Right Implementation of the Constitution on the Sacred Liturgy *Varietates legitimae* (January 25, 1994). *Acta Apostolicae Sedis* 87 (1995): 288–314.

Cross, F.L. "Pre-Leonine Elements in the Proper of the Roman Mass". *Journal of Theological Studies* 50 (1949): 191–97.

Crystal, D. "Liturgical Language in a Sociolinguistic Perspective". In *Language and the Worship of the Church*, edited by D. Jasper and R.C.D. Jasper, 120–46. Studies in Literature and Religion. Basingstoke: Macmillan, 1990.

Deléani, S. "Les caractères du latin chrétien". In *Il latino e i cristiani: Un bilancio all'inizio del terzo millennio*, edited by E. dal Covolo and M. Sodi, 3–25. Monumenta Studia Instrumenta Liturgica 17. Vatican City: Libreria Editrice Vaticana, 2002.

Dekkers, E. *Tertullianus en de geschiedenis der liturgie*. Catholica 6, 2. Brussels: De Kinkhoren; Amsterdam: Desclée de Brouwer, 1947.

De Zan, R. "How to Interpret a Collect". In *Appreciating the Collect: An Irenic Methodology*, edited by J.G. Leachman and D.P.

McCarthy, 57–82. Liturgiam Aestimare: Appreciating the Liturgy 1. Farnborough: Saint Michael's Abbey Press, 2008.

Díaz Patri, G. "Poetry in the Latin Liturgy". In *The Genius of the Roman Liturgy: Historical Diversity and Spiritual Reach: Proceedings of the 2006 Oxford CIEL Colloquium*, edited by U. M. Lang, 45–82. Chicago: Hillenbrand Books, 2010.

Díaz y Díaz, M. C. "El latín de la liturgia hispánica: Notas introductorias". In *Estudios sobre la liturgia mozárabe*, edited by J. Rivera Recio, 55–87. Toledo: Diputación Provincial, 1965.

Documents on the Liturgy 1963–1979: Conciliar, Papal, and Curial Texts. Collegeville, Minn.: Liturgical Press, 1982.

Duffy, E. "The Catholic Church on the Eve of the New Millennium". *Catholic Medical Quarterly* 50 (2000): 42–47, and 51 (2001): 29–34. Also available at: http://www.christendom-awake.org/pages/duffy/newmill.html.

______. "Rewriting the Liturgy: The Theological Implications of Translation". In *Beyond the Prosaic: Renewing the Liturgical Movement*, edited by S. Caldecott, 97–126. Edinburgh: T&T Clark, 1998. (Also published in *New Blackfriars* 78 [1997]: 4–27.)

Eizenhöfer, L. *Canon Missae romanae: Pars altera: Textus propinqui*. Rerum Ecclesiasticarum Documenta. Series minor. Subsidia studiorum 7. Rome: Herder, 1966.

Eliot T. S. "Dante". In *Selected Prose of T. S. Eliot*, edited by F. Kermode, 205–30. London: Faber and Faber, 1975.

Ellebracht, M. P. *Remarks on the Vocabulary of the Ancient Orations in the Missale Romanum*. Latinitas Christianorum Primaeva 18. 2nd ed. Nijmegen and Utrecht: Dekker & Van de Vegt, 1966.

Engberding, H. "Die Kunstprosa des eucharistischen Hochgebetes der griechischen Gregoriusliturgie". In *Mullus: Festschrift Theodor Klauser*. Jahrbuch für Antike und Christentum. Ergänzungsband 1. Münster: Aschendorff, 1964, 100–110.

English-Latin Roman Missal for the United States of America: Containing the Mass Text from the Roman Missal and the Prayers of the Celebrant together with the Ordinary of the Mass from the English-Latin Sacramentary. English Translations Approved by the National Conference of Bishops of the United States of America and Confirmed by the Apostolic See. New York: Benziger Brothers, 1966.

Ferrua, A. "Latino cristiano antico". *La Civiltà Cattolica* 95 (1944): 35–38, 237–44, 370–77.

Fögen, T. *Patrii sermonis egestas: Einstellungen lateinischer Autoren zu ihrer Muttersprache.* Beiträge zur Altertumskunde 150. Munich and Leipzig: K. G. Saur, 2000.

Foley, M. P. "The Mystic Meaning of the *Missale Romanum*". *Antiphon* 13 (2009): 103–25.

Fortescue, A. *The Mass: A Study of the Roman Liturgy.* 2nd ed. London: Longmans, Green and Co., 1950.

Fredouille, J.-C. "Latin chrétien ou latin tardif?" *Recherches Augustiniennes* 29 (1996): 5–23.

García de la Fuente, O. *Latín bíblico y latín cristiano.* 2nd rev. and enlarged ed. Madrid: Ed. CEES, 1994.

Gelston, A. *The Eucharistic Prayer of Addai and Mari.* Oxford: Clarendon Press, 1992.

______. "The Meaning of *šl'* in Theodore of Mopsuestia's Sixteenth Catechetical Lecture and the Silent recitation of the Eucharistic Prayer". *Journal of Theological Studies*, n.s., 60 (2009): 191–92.

Ghellinck, J. de. "Latin chrétien ou langue latine des chrétiens?" *Les études classiques* 8 (1939): 449–78.

Goessling, F. *Adrians* ΕΙΣΑΓΩΓΗ ΕΙΣ ΤΑΣ ΘΕΙΑΣ ΓΡΑΦΑΣ *aus neu aufgefundenen Handschriften herausgegeben, übersetzt und erläutert.* Berlin: Reuther, 1887.

Grillmeier, A. *Christ in Christian Tradition*. Vol. 2, pt. 2, *The Church of Constantinople in the Sixth Century*. Translated by J. Cawte and P. Allen. London: Mowbray; Louisville, Ky.: Westminster John Knox Press, 1995.

Gy, P.-M. "Avancées du traité de l'eucharistie de s. Thomas dans la *Somme* par rapport aux *Sentences*". *Revue des sciences philosophiques et théologiques* 77 (1993): 219–28.

______. "L'office du Corpus Christi et s. Thomas d'Aquin. État d'une recherche". *Revue des sciences philosophiques et théologiques* 64 (1980): 491–507.

Haessly, M. G. *Rhetoric in the Sunday Collects of the Roman Missal, with Introduction, Text, Commentary and Translation*. Cleveland: Ursuline College for Women, 1938.

Hammerstaedt, J., and P. Terbuyken. "Improvisation". *Reallexikon für Antike und Christentum* 17 (1996): 1212–84.

Hänggi, A., and I. Pahl. *Prex eucharistica*. Vol. 1: *Textus e variis liturgiis antiquioribus selecti*. 3rd ed. Spicilegium Friburgense 12. Fribourg: Universitätsverlag, 1998.

Harnack, A. von. *The Mission and Expansion of Christianity in the First Three Centuries*. Translated and edited by J. Moffatt. 2 vols. 2nd ed. London: Williams & Norgate, 1908.

Hedrick, C. W. *History and Silence: Purge and Rehabilitation of Memory in Late Antiquity*. Austin: University of Texas Press, 2000.

Hickson, F. *Roman Prayer Language: Livy and the Aeneid of Virgil*. Stuttgart: Teubner, 1993.

Hock, H. *Principles of Historical Linguistics*. Berlin, New York, and Amsterdam: Mouton de Gruyter, 1988.

Humbrecht, T.-D. "L'Eucharistie, 'représentation' du sacrifice du Christ, selon saint Thomas". *Revue Thomiste* 98 (1998): 355–86.

Jammo, S. Y. H. "Gabriel Qatraya et son commentaire sur la liturgie chaldéenne". *Orientalia Christiana Periodica* 32 (1966): 39–52.

______. *La structure de la messe chaldéenne du début jusqu'à l'anaphore.* Orientalia Christiana Analecta 207. Rome: Pontificium Institutum Orientalium Studiorum, 1979.

Jeanes, G. "Early Latin Parallels to the Roman Canon? Possible References to a Eucharistic Prayer in Zeno of Verona". *Journal of Theological Studies*, n.s., 37 (1986): 427–31.

John Paul II, Apostolic Letter *Dominicae cenae* (February 24, 1980). *Acta Apostolicae Sedis* 72 (1980): 113–48. English translation: http://www.vatican.va/holy_father/john_paul_ii/letters/documents/hf_jp-ii_let_24021980_dominicae-cenae_en.html.

Jungmann, J. A. *Missarum Sollemnia: Eine genetische Erklärung der römischen Messe.* 2 vols. 5th ed. Vienna: Herder, 1962.

Kamesar, A. "Ambrose, Philo and the Presence of Art in the Bible". *Journal of Early Christian Studies* 9 (2001): 73–103.

Klauser, T. "Der Übergang der römischen Kirche von der griechischen zur lateinischen Liturgiesprache". In *Miscellanea Giovanni Mercati.* Vol. 1: *Bibbia, letteratura cristiana antica*, 467–82. Studi e testi 121. Vatican City: Biblioteca Apostolica Vaticana, 1946.

Klöckener, M. "Das eucharistische Hochgebet in der nordafrikanischen Liturgie der christlichen Spätantike". In *Prex eucharistica.* Vol. 3: *Studia.* Part 1*: Ecclesia antiqua et occidentalis*, edited by A. Gerhards, H. Brakmann, and M. Klöckener, 43–128. Spicilegium Friburgense 42. Fribourg: Academic Press, 2005.

______. "Zeitgemäßes Beten: Meßorationen als Zeugnisse einer sich wandelnden Kultur und Spiritualität". In *Bewahren und Erneuern: Studien zur Meßliturgie: Festschrift für Hans Bernhard Meyer SJ zum 70. Geburtstag*, edited by R. Meßner, E. Nagel, and R. Pacik, 114–42. Innsbrucker theologische Studien 42. Innsbruck and Vienna: Tyrolia, 1995.

Kolbaba, T. M. *The Byzantine Lists: Errors of the Latins*. Illinois Medieval Studies. Chicago: University of Illinois Press, 2000.

Kretschmar, G. "Die frühe Geschichte der Jerusalemer Liturgie". *Jahrbuch für Liturgik und Hymnologie* 2 (1956–1957): 22–46.

______. *Studien zur frühchristlichen Trinitätstheologie*. Beiträge zur historischen Theologie 21. Tübingen: J. C. B. Mohr, 1956.

Labriolle, P. "Salvator". *Archivum Latinitatis Mediae Aetatis* 14 (1939): 23–36.

Lafferty, M. K. "Translating Faith from Greek to Latin: Romanitas and Christianitas in Late Fourth-Century Rome and Milan". *Journal of Early Christian Studies* 11 (2003): 21–62.

Lampe, P. *Christians at Rome in the First Two Centuries: From Paul to Valentinus*. Translated by M. Steinhauser and edited by M. D. Johnson. London: Continuum, 2006.

Lane Fox, R. *Pagans and Christians*. London: Viking, 1986.

Lang, A. P. "Anklänge an eine Heilig Geist Oration in einem Sermo Leos des Grossen auf die Fastenzeit". *Sacris Erudiri* 23 (1978–1979): 143–70.

______. "Anklänge an liturgische Texte in Epiphaniesermonen Leos des Grossen". *Sacris Erudiri* 10 (1958): 43–126.

______. "Anklänge an Orationen der Ostervigil in Sermonen Leos des Grossen". *Sacris Erudiri* 13 (1962): 281–325.

______. "Anklänge an Orationen der Ostervigil in Sermonen Leos des Grossen". *Sacris Erudiri* 18 (1967–1968): 5–119.

______. "Anklänge an Orationen der Ostervigil in Sermonen Leos des Grossen". *Sacris Erudiri* 27 (1984): 129–49.

______. "Anklänge an Orationen der Ostervigil in Sermonen Leos des Grossen". *Sacris Erudiri* 28 (1985): 155–381.

______. "Leo der Große und die Dreifaltigkeitspräfation". *Sacris Erudiri* 9 (1957): 116–62.

______. "Leo der Grosse und die liturgischen Gebetstexte des Epiphaniefestes". *Sacris Erudiri* 14 (1963): 3*–22*.

______. "Leo der Grosse und die liturgischen Texte des Oktavtages von Epiphanie". *Sacris Erudiri* 11 (1960): 12–135.

______. *Leo der Grosse und die Texte des Altgelasianums mit Berücksichtigung des Sacramentarium Leonianum und des Sacramentarium Gregorianum*. Steyl: Steyler Verlagsbuchhandlung, 1957.

Lang, U. M. "Found in Translation: The 'Sacral Vernacular' of the New English Translation of the Roman Missal". *The Priest: The Journal of Australian Confraternity of Catholic Clergy* 25 (2010): 20–27, 33.

______. "Rhetoric of Salvation: The Origins of Latin as the Language of the Roman Liturgy". In *The Genius of the Roman Liturgy: Historical Diversity and Spiritual Reach: Proceedings of the 2006 Oxford CIEL Colloquium*, edited by U. M. Lang, 22–44. Chicago: Hillenbrand Books, 2010.

Leachman, J. G. "History of Collect Studies". In *Appreciating the Collect: An Irenic Methodology*, edited by J. G. Leachman and D. P. McCarthy, 1–25. Liturgiam Aestimare: Appreciating the Liturgy 1. Farnborough: Saint Michael's Abbey Press, 2008.

Léonas, A. *L'aube des traducteurs: De l'hébreu au grec: Traducteurs et lecteurs de la Bible des Septante IIIe s. av. J.-C–IVe s. apr. J.-C.* Initiations bibliques. Paris: Cerf, 2007.

______. *Recherches sur le langage de la Septante*. Orbis Biblicus et Orientalis 211. Fribourg: Academic Press; Göttingen: Vandenhoeck & Ruprecht, 2005.

Levering, M. *Sacrifice and Community: Jewish Offering and Christian Eucharist.* Oxford: Blackwell, 2005.

Lohfink, N. "Liturgische Bibelverdunstung: Die Bibel-Intertextualität bei der Verdeutschung der lateinischen Liturgie". *Stimmen der Zeit* 218 (2000): 247–59.

Lunn-Rockliffe, S. *Ambrosiaster's Political Theology.* Oxford Early Christian Studies. Oxford: Oxford University Press, 2007.

Macomber, W. F. "An Anaphora Prayer Composed by Theodore of Mopsuestia". *Parole de l'Orient* 6–7 (1975–1976): 341–47.

Mack, P. "Rhetoric and Liturgy". In *Language and the Worship of the Church*, edited by D. Jasper and R. C. D. Jasper, 82–109. Studies in Literature and Religion. Basingstoke: Macmillan, 1990.

Manns, F. "L'origine judéo-chrétienne de la prière 'Unde et memores' du Canon Romain". *Ephemerides Liturgicae* 101 (1987): 60–68.

———. "Une Prière judéo-chrétienne dans le Canon Romain". *Antonianum* 54 (1979): 3–9.

Marcus, R. *The End of Ancient Christianity.* Cambridge: Cambridge University Press, 1990.

Marin, M. "La prosa d'arte cristiana latina". In *Il latino e i cristiani: Un bilancio all'inizio del terzo millennio*, edited by E. dal Covolo and M. Sodi, 29–54. Monumenta Studia Instrumenta Liturgica 17. Vatican City: Libreria Editrice Vaticana, 2002.

Markschies, C. "Wer schrieb die sogenannte Traditio Apostolica? Neue Beobachtungen und Hypothesen zu einer kaum lösbaren Frage aus der altkirchlichen Literaturgeschichte". In *Tauffragen und Bekenntnis: Studien zur sogenannten "Traditio Apostolica", zu den "Interrogationes de fide" und zum "Römischen Glaubensbekenntnis"*, by C. Markschies, W. Kinzig, and M. Vinzent, 1–79. Arbeiten zur Kirchengeschichte 74. Berlin and New York: de Gruyter, 1999.

Marshall, B.D. "The Whole Mystery of Our Salvation: Saint Thomas Aquinas on the Eucharist as Sacrifice". In *Rediscovering Aquinas and the Sacraments: Studies in Sacramental Theology*, edited by M. Levering and M. Dauphinais, 39–64. Chicago: Hillenbrand, 2009.

McManus, D. "Translation Theory in *Liturgiam authenticam*". In *Benedict XVI and the Sacred Liturgy: Proceedings of the First Fota International Liturgy Conference 2008*, edited by N.J. Roy and J.E. Rutherford, 116–31. Fota Liturgy Series. Dublin: Four Courts Press, 2010.

Meeks, W. *The First Urban Christians: The Social World of the Apostle Paul*. New Haven: Yale University Press, 1983.

Meister, K. *Die homerische Kunstsprache*. Preisschriften der Fürstlich-Jablonowskischen Gesellschaft 48. Leipzig: Teubner, 1921.

Metzger, M. "À propos des règlements ecclésiastiques et de la prétendue *Tradition apostolique*". *Revue des sciences religieuses* 66 (1992): 249–61.

Missale Romanum ex decreto Sacrosancti Concilii Tridentini restitutum Pii V Pont. Max. iussu editum. Rome: Apud heredes Bartholomei Faletti, Joannem Variscum & socios, 1570.

Missale Romanum ex decreto SS. Concilii Tridentini restitutum Summorum Pontificum cura recognitum. Editio typica. Vatican City: Typis Polyglottis Vaticanis, 1962.

Missale Romanum ex decreto Sacrosancti Oecumenici Concilii Vaticani II instauratum auctoritate Pauli PP. VI promulgatum. Editio typica. Vatican City: Typis Polyglottis Vaticani, 1970.

Missale Romanum ex decreto Sacrosancti Oecumenici Concilii Vaticani II instauratum auctoritate Pauli PP. VI promulgatum Ioannis Pauli PP. II cura recognitum. Editio typica tertia, reimpressio emendata, Vatican City: Typis Vaticanis, 2002.

Mohlberg, L. C. *Liber Sacramentorum Romanae Aeclesiae Ordinis Anni Circuli*. 3rd ed. Rerum Ecclesiasticarum Documenta. Series maior. Fontes IV. Rome: Herder, 1981.

Mohrmann, C. "Comment saint Augustin s'est familiarisé avec le latin des chrétiens". *Études sur le latin des chrétiens* 1:383–89. (Originally published in: *Augustinus Magister I. Congrès International Augustinien*. Paris, 1954. 111–16.)

———. "Les emprunts grecs dans la latinité chrétienne". In *Études sur le latin des chrétiens* 3:127–45. (Originally published in *Vigiliae Christianae* 4 [1950]: 193–211.)

———. "L'étude de la latinité chrétienne: État de la question, méthodes, résultats". In *Études sur le latin des chrétiens* 1:83–102. (Originally published in: *Conférences de l'Institut de linguistique de l'Université de Paris* 10 [1950/1951]: 125–41.)

———. *Études sur le latin des chrétiens*. 4 vols. Storia e letteratura 65, 87, 103, 143. Rome: Edizioni di Storia e Letteratura, 1961–1977.

———. "The Ever-Recurring Problem of Language in the Church". In *Études sur le latin des chrétiens* 4:143–59. (Originally published in *Theology of Renewal*, vol. 2. Montreal, 1968. 204–20.)

———. "Le latin commun et le latin des chrétiens". In *Études sur le latin des chrétiens* 3:13–24. (Originally published in *Vigiliae Christianae* 1 [1947]: 1–12.)

———. "Linguistic Problems in the Early Christian Church." In *Études sur le latin des chrétiens* 3:171–196. (Originally published in *Vigitiae Christianae* II [1957]: 11–36.)

———. *Liturgical Latin: Its Origins and Character: Three Lectures*. London: Burns & Oates, 1959.

———. "The New Latin Psalter: Its Diction and Style". In *Études sur le latin des chrétiens* 2:109–31. (Originally published in *The American Benedictine Review* 5 [1953]: 7–33.)

______. "Problèmes stylistiques dans la littérature latine chrétienne". In *Études sur le latin des chrétiens* 3:147–70. (Originally published in *Vigiliae Christianae* 9 [1955]: 222–46.)

______. "Quelques observations sur l'évolution stylistique du Canon de la Messe romain". In *Études sur le latin des chrétiens* 3:227–44. (Originally published in *Vigiliae Christianae* 4 [1950]: 1–19.)

______. "*Rationabilis*—λογικός". In *Études sur le latin des chrétiens* 1:179–87. (Originally published in *Mélanges Fernand de Visscher*, vol. 4. Brussels, 1950 = *Revue International des Droits de l'Antiquité* 5 [1950]: 225–34.)

______. "Saint Augustin écrivain". In *Études sur le latin des chrétiens* 2:247–75. (Originally published in *Recherches Augustiniennes* 1 [1958]: 43–66.)

______. "Sur l'histoire de Praefari-Praefatio". In *Études sur le latin des chrétiens* 3:291–305. (Originally published in *Vigiliae Christianae* 7 [1953]: 1–15.)

Moore, G. "The Vocabulary of the Collects: Retrieving a Biblical Heritage". In *Appreciating the Collect: An Irenic Methodology*, edited by J. G. Leachman and D. P. McCarthy, 175–95. Liturgiam Aestimare: Appreciating the Liturgy 1. Farnborough: Saint Michael's Abbey Press, 2008.

Moreton, M. J. "Rethinking the Origin of the Roman Canon". *Studia Patristica* 26 (1993): 63–66.

Mowinckel, S. *Religion und Kultus*. Translated by A. Schauer. Göttingen: Vandenhoeck & Ruprecht, 1953.

Nichols, A. *Looking at the Liturgy: A Critical View of Its Contemporary Form*. San Francisco: Ignatius Press, 1996.

Nida, E. A. *Toward a Science of Translating, with Special Reference to Principles and Procedures Involved in Bible Translating*. Leiden: Brill, 1964.

Norden, E. *Die antike Kunstprosa vom VI. Jahrhundert v. Chr. bis in die Zeit der Renaissance*. 2 vols. 2nd ed. Leipzig: Teubner, 1909.

O'Donnell, J.J. *Augustine, Confessions: Introduction, Text, and Commentary*. 3 vols. Oxford: Clarendon Press, 1992.

Oroz Reta, J., ed. *Actas del I Simposio de Latín Cristiano*. Bibliotheca Salmanticensis; Estudios, 130 = *Helmantica* 40 (1989). Salamanca: Univ. Pontificia, 1990.

O'Toole, J. M. *The Faithful: A History of Catholics in America*. Cambridge, Mass.: Belknap Press, 2008.

Palmer, L. R. *The Latin Language*. London: Faber and Faber, 1954.

Paul VI. *Address to Translators of Liturgical Texts* (November 10, 1965). *Acta Apostolicae Sedis* 57 (1965): 967–70.

______. Apostolic letter given Motu Proprio *Sacram liturgiam* (January 25, 1964). *Acta Apostolicae Sedis* 56 (1964): 139–44.

Pecklers, K. *Dynamic Equivalence: The Living Language of Christian Worship*. Collegeville: Liturgical Press, 2003.

Pieper, J. *In Search of the Sacred*. Translated by L. Krauth. San Francisco: Ignatius Press, 1991.

______. *Religionsphilosophische Schriften*. Edited by B. Wald. Werke 7. Hamburg: Felix Meiner, 2000.

Pietri, C. "Damase évêque de Rome". In *Saecularia Damasiana: Atti del convegno internazionale per il XVI centenario della morte di Papa Damaso I (11–12–384—10/12–12–1984)*, 29–58. Studi di antichità cristiana 39. Vatican City: Pontificio Istituto di Archeologia Cristiana, 1986.

Pius XII. Encyclical on the Sacred Liturgy *Mediator Dei* (November 20, 1947). *Acta Apostolicae Sedis* 39 (1947): 521–95; English translation: http://www.vatican.va/holy_father/pius_xii/encyclicals/documents/hf_p-xii_enc_20111947_mediator-dei_en.html.

Pontifical Commission *Ecclesia Dei*. Instruction on the Application of the Apostolic Letter *Summorum Pontificum* given Motu Proprio *Universae Ecclesiae* (April 30, 2011). *L'Osservatore Romano*, May 14, 2011, 4–5; English translation: http://www.vatican.va/roman_curia/pontifical_commissions/ecclsdei/documents/rc_com_ecclsdei_doc_20110430_istr-universae-ecclesiae_en.html.

Pontifical Council for Legislative Texts. "Nota Esplicativa X: La natura giuridica e l'estensione della "recognitio" della Santa Sede". *Communicationes* 38 (2006): 10–17.

Preghiere dell'umanità: Testi scelti e presentati da P. Miquel and M. Perrini. Translated by P. Brognoli and M. Perrrini. Brescia: Queriniana, 1993.

Pristas, L. "The Orations of the Vatican II Missals: Policies for Revision". *Communio (U.S.)* 30 (2003): 621–53.

______. "The Post-Vatican II Revision of the Lenten Collects". In *Ever Directed Towards the Lord: The Love of God in the Liturgy of the Eucharist Past Present, and Hoped For*, edited by U. M. Lang, 62–89. London: T&T Clark (Continuum), 2007.

Quoëx, F. "Thomas d'Aquin, mystagogue: l'*Expositio Missae* de la *Somme de théologie* (IIIa, q. 83, a. 4–5)". *Revue Thomiste* 105 (2005): 179–225 and 435–72.

Ratcliff, E. C. "The Institution Narrative of the Roman Canon Missae: Its Beginning and Early Background". In *Liturgical Studies*, edited by A. H. Couratin and D. H. Tripp, 49–65. London: SPCK, 1976. (Originally published in *Studia Patristica* 2 [1957]: 64–82.)

______. "A Note on the Anaphoras described in the Liturgical Homilies of Narsai". In *Liturgical Studies*, edited by A. H. Couratin and D. H. Tripp, 66–79. London: SPCK, 1976. (Originally published in *Biblical and Patristic Studies in Memory of Robert*

Pierce Casay, edited by J. N. Birdsall and R. W. Thomson, 235–49. Freiburg: Herder, 1963.)

———, and A. H. Couratin. "The Roman *Canon Missae*: Its Beginnings and Early Background". In *Liturgical Studies*, edited by A. H. Couratin and D. H. Tripp, 91–107. London: SPCK, 1976. (Originally published in *Journal of Ecclesiastical History* [1969]: 211–24.)

Ratzinger, J. "Assessment and Future Prospects". In *Looking Again at the Question of the Liturgy with Cardinal Ratzinger: Proceedings of the 2001 Fontgombault Liturgical Conference*, edited by A. Reid, 145–53. Farnborough: Saint Michael's Abbey Press, 2003.

———. "Bilan et Perspectives". In *Theologie der Liturgie: Die sakramentale Begründung christlicher Existenz*, 657–82. Gesammelte Schriften 11. Freiburg: Herder, 2008.

———. "Communication and Culture: New Methods of Evangelization in the Third Millennium". In *On the Way to Jesus Christ*. Translated by M. J. Miller, 42–52. San Francisco: Ignatius Press, 2005.

———. "Preface". In *The Organic Development of the Liturgy: The Principles of Liturgical Reform and Their Relation to the Twentieth-Century Liturgical Movement Prior to the Second Vatican Council*, by A. Reid, 9–13. 2nd ed. San Francisco: Ignatius Press, 2005.

———. *The Spirit of the Liturgy*. Translated by J. Saward. San Francisco: Ignatius Press, 2000.

———. "Um die Erneuerung der Liturgie: Antwort auf Reiner Kaczynski". *Stimmen der Zeit* 219 (2001): 837–43.

Regan, P. "The Collect in Context". In *Appreciating the Collect: An Irenic Methodology*, edited by J. G. Leachman and D. P. McCarthy, 83–103. Liturgiam Aestimare: Appreciating the Liturgy 1. Farnborough: Saint Michael's Abbey Press, 2008.

Reutter, U. *Damasus, Bischof von Rom (366–384): Leben und Werk.* Studien und Texte zu Antike und Christentum 55. Tübingen: Mohr Siebeck, 2009.

Rico, C. "L'art de la traduction chez Saint Jérôme: La Vulgate à l'aune de la Néovulgate: L'exemple du quatrième évangile". *Revue des Études Latines* 83 (2006): 194–218.

______. "La traduction du sens littéral chez saint Jérôme". In *Le sens littéral des Écritures*, edited by O.-T. Venard, 171–218. Collection Lectio Divina, Hors Série. Paris: Cerf, 2009.

Rives, J. *Religion and Authority in Roman Carthage from Augustus to Constantine.* Oxford: Clarendon, 1995.

Robinson, J. *The Mass and Modernity: Walking to Heaven Backward.* San Francisco: Ignatius Press, 2005.

Roche, A. "Search for Truth and Poetry". *The Tablet*, August 5, 2006, 10–11.

Roman Missal: Missale Romanum ex decreto Sacrosancti Concilii Tridentini restitutum Summorum Pontificum cura recognitum cum versionibus lingua anglica exaratis et a coetu episcoporum Civitatum Foederatum America Septentrionalis rite approbatis actis ab Apostolica Sede confirmatis. New York: Benziger Brothers, 1964.

Roman Missal: Renewed by Decree of the Most Holy Second Ecumenical Council of the Vatican, Promulgated by Authority of Pope Paul VI and Revised at the Direction of Pope John Paul II. Totowa, N.J.: Catholic Book Publishing, 2011.

Roman Missal: Revised by Decree of the Second Vatican Council and Published by Authority of Pope Paul VI. London: Collins Liturgical, 1974.

Rose, E. "Liturgical Latin in the Bobbio Missal". In *The Bobbio Missal: Liturgy and Religious Culture in Merovingian Gaul*, edited by Y. Hen and R. Meens, 67–78. Cambridge Studies in

Palaeography and Codicology. Cambridge: Cambridge University Press, 2004.

______. "Liturgical Latin in the *Missale Gothicum* (Vat. Reg. Lat. 317)". *Sacris Erudiri* 42 (2003): 97–121.

Rose, H. G. E., ed. *Missale gothicum e codice Vaticano Reginensi latino 317 editum*. CCSL 159D. Turnhout: Brepols, 2005.

Roy, N.J. "The Roman Canon: *deësis* in euchological form". In *Benedict XVI and the Sacred Liturgy*, edited by N.J. Roy and J.E. Rutherford, 181–99. Dublin: Four Courts Press, 2010.

Rubio, G. "Semitic Influence in the History of Latin Syntax". In *New Perspectives on Historical Latin Syntax*, edited by P. Bald and P. Cuzzolin, 1:195–239. Trends in Linguistics: Studies & Monographs 180.1. Berlin and New York, 2009.

Sacred Congregation of Rites. Instruction for the Right Implementation of the Constitution on the Sacred Liturgy *Inter oecumenici* (September 26, 1964). *Acta Apostolicae Sedis* 56 (1964): 877–900.

______. Second Instruction for the Right Implementation of the Constitution on the Sacred Liturgy *Tres abhinc annos* (May 4, 1967). *Acta Apostolicae Sedis* 59 (1967): 442–48.

Saxer, V. "'Figura Corporis et Sanguinis Domini': une formule eucharistique des premiers siècles chez Tertullian, Hippolyte et Ambroise". *Rivista di archeologia cristiana* 48 (1971): 65–89. (= *Pères saints et culte chrétien dans l'Église des premiers siècles*. Collected Studies Series 448. Aldershot: Variorum, 1994, no. IV.)

Schmidt, H. A. P. *Liturgie et langue vulgaire: Le problème de la langue liturgique chez les premiers Réformateurs et au Concile de Trente*. Analecta Gregoriana 53. Rome: Apud Aedes Unversitatis Gregorianae, 1950.

Schwartz, E. *Zur Kirchenpolitik Justinians*. Sitzungsberichte der Bayerischen Akademie der Wissenschaften zu München,

Philosophisch-Historische Abteilung 1940/2. Munich: Beck, 1940.

Second Vatican Council, Constitution on the Sacred Liturgy *Sacrosanctum concilium* (December 4, 1963). *Acta Apostolicae Sedis* 56 (1964): 97–134; English translation: http://www.vatican.va/archive/hist_councils/ii_vatican_council/documents/vat-ii_const_19631204_sacrosanctum-concilium_en.html.

Senn, F. C. *The People's Work: A Social History of the Liturgy*. Minneapolis: Fortress Press, 2006.

Sheerin, D. "Christian and Biblical Latin". In *Medieval Latin: An Introduction and Bibliographical Guide*, edited by F. A. C. Mantello and A. G. Rigg, 137–56. Washington, D.C.: Catholic University of America Press, 1996.

Shepherd, H. "The Liturgical Reform of Damasus I". In *Kyriakon: Festschrift Johannes Quasten*, edited by P. Granfield and J. A. Jungmann, 2:847–63. Münster: Aschendorff, 1970.

Spaemann, R. "Europa—Wertegemeinschaft oder Rechtsordnung?". *Transit—Europäische Revue* 21/2001: 172–85.

Steimer, B. *Vertex traditionis: Die Gattung der altchristlichen Kirchenordnungen*. Beihefte zur Zeitschrift für die neutestamentliche Wissenschaft 63. Berlin and New York: de Gruyter, 1992.

Stock, A. *Liturgie und Poesie: Zur Sprache des Gottesdienstes*. Kevelaer: Butzon & Bercker, 2010.

Thompson, A. *Cities of God: The Religion of the Italian Communes 1125–1325*. University Park, Pa.: Pennsylvania State University Press, 2005.

Thomson, F. J. "SS. Cyril and Methodius and a Mythical Western Heresy: Trilinguism: A Contribution to the Study of Patristic and Mediaeval Theories of Sacred Languages". *Analecta Bollandiana* 110 (1992): 67–122.

Torrell, J.-P. *Saint Thomas Aquinas*. Vol. 1: *The Person and His Work*. Translated by R. Royal. Washington, D.C.: Catholic University of America Press, 1996.

Trapp, W. *Vorgeschichte und Ursprung der liturgischen Bewegung vorwiegend in Hinsicht auf das deutsche Sprachgebiet*. Regensburg, 1940; repr., Münster: Antiquariat Stenderhoff, 1979.

Van Slyke, D. G. "The Changing Meanings of *sacramentum*: Historical Sketches". *Antiphon* 11 (2007): 245–79.

Vogel, C. *Medieval Liturgy: An Introduction to the Sources*. Revised and translated by W. G. Storey and N. K. Rasmussen. Washington, D.C.: Pastoral Press, 1986.

Vonier, A. *A Key to the Doctrine of the Eucharist*. London: Burns, Oates & Washbourne, 1925.

Ward, A. "The Orations for Ash Wednesday in the Present Roman Missal". *Notitiae* 44 (2007): 45–64.

______, and C. Johnson, eds. *The Prefaces of the Roman Missal: A Source Compendium with Concordance and Indices*. Rome: Tipografia Poliglotta Vaticana, 1989.

Watts, E.J. *City and School in Late Antique Athens and Alexandria*. The Transformation of the Classical Heritage 41. Berkeley: University of California Press, 2006.

Westermayer, H. *Die Brandenburgisch-Nürnbergische Kirchenvisitation und Kirchenordnung 1528–1533: Auf Grund der Akten dargestellt*. Erlangen: Junge, 1894.

Wielockx, R. "Au sujet du commentaire de saint Thomas sur le 'Corpus Paulinum': Critique littéraire". in *L'interpretazione di san Tommaso delle dottrine di san Paolo: Atti della IX Sessione Plenaria, 19–21 giugno 2009* (Doctor communis), 150–84. Vatican City: Pontificia Academia Sancti Thomae Aquinatis, 2009.

Wilken, R. L. "The Church as Culture". *First Things* 142 (April 2004): 31–37.

______. "The Church's Way of Speaking". *First Things* 154 (August/September 2005): 27–31.

Willis, G. G. "The Connection of the Prayers of the Roman Canon". In *Essays in Early Roman Liturgy*, 121–33. Alcuin Club Collections 46. London: SPCK, 1964.

______. *A History of Early Roman Liturgy to the Death of Pope Gregory the Great.* Henry Bradshaw Society, Subsidia 1. London: Boydell Press, 1994.

______. "St Gregory the Great and the Lord's Prayer in the Roman Mass". In *Further Essays in Early Roman Liturgy*, 175–88. Alcuin Club Collections 50. London: SPCK, 1968.

______. "The Variable Prayers of the Roman Mass". In *Further Essays in Early Roman Liturgy*, 91–129. Alcuin Club Collections 50. London: SPCK, 1968.

Wischmeyer, W. *Von Golgatha zum Ponte Molle: Studien zur Sozialgeschichte der Kirche im dritten Jahrhundert.* Forschungen zur Kirchen- und Dogmengeschichte 49. Göttingen: Vandenhoeck & Ruprecht, 1992.

Wright, R. "Foreword". In *Vulgar Latin*, by J. Herman, translated by R. Wright, ix–x. University Park, Pa.: Pennsylvania State University Press, 2000.

______. *Late Latin and Early Romance in Spain and Carolingian France.* ARCA 8. Liverpool: Francis Cairns, 1982.

______. *A Sociophilological Study of Late Latin.* Utrecht Studies in Medieval Literacy 10. Turnhout: Brepols, 2002.

Yarnold, E. *Cyril of Jerusalem.* The Early Church Fathers. London and New York: Routledge, 2000.